Department of Education and Science
Department of Education for Northern
Welsh Office

Assessment of Performance Unit

# Mathematical Development

## Secondary Survey Report No. 3

by
D D Foxman
R M Martini
P Mitchell

Report on the 1980 secondary survey from the National Foundation for Educational Research in England and Wales to the Department of Education and Science, Department of Education for Northern Ireland and the Welsh Office.

London
Her Majesty's Stationery Office

**ISBN 0 11 270518 9**

# Contents

# Tables

# Figures

# Acknowledgements

The monitoring team at the NFER would like to thank the large number of people who played a part in enabling the survey reported here to take place and who contributed to the work involved in producing this report.

We are again indebted to the schools which participated. Many of the heads and teachers in these schools made helpful comments on the content and presentation of the test materials. We should also like to thank the LEAs who nominated teachers to be testers in the practical mathematics survey. These teachers (listed in Appendix 3) wrote extremely valuable critiques of the tests which will make a substantial contribution to the development of this innovative form of assessment.

The monitoring surveys require careful administrative and co-ordinating procedures. These were the responsibility of Mrs B. Bloomfield as head of the Monitoring Services Unit and her staff based at the NFER. They were responsible for all matters pertaining to contact with the LEAs and the schools which took part in the survey. The statistical analysis of the results was guided by members of the NFER Technical Committee and, in particular, by Mr B. Sexton and his colleagues Mr P. Smedley and Mr J. Simpson.

A number of colleagues at the NFER, members of the Monitoring Group, made helpful comments on the initial draft of the report as did Dr I. Wells of the Northern Ireland Council for Educational Research. Members of APU Committees, the Steering Group on Mathematics, the Advisory Group on Statistics and the Consultative Committee, have read and discussed the initial draft and their recommendations have greatly contributed to the final draft of the report.

Successive versions of the text and various amendments have been typed with much patience and skill by our secretary Mrs J. Pengilly and were assembled by our clerical assistant Mrs R. James.

# Summary of report

1 This report is the third in a series which together will build-up a national picture of the mathematical performance of 15 year old pupils in England, Wales and Northern Ireland. It covers the survey carried out in 1980 and includes some references to the results of similar surveys of 11 year olds carried out earlier. As in all APU surveys, individual pupils, schools or local education authorities are not identified.

## Secondary survey No 3 (Chapter 1)

2 Written tests were administered to a representative national sample of approximately 13,300 15 year old pupils in England, Wales and Northern Ireland. The tests included many of the questions from previous surveys, together with 150 new items. A sub-sample of 1140 pupils also took a practical test and a separate sub-sample of 1073 pupils completed an attitude questionnaire. A further sub-sample of the main sample took pilot written tests concerned with problem solving. The written tests of concepts and skills emphasised certain aspects of mathematics at the expense of others: to achieve this, the sub-category Rate and ratio was omitted as a separate category, and the sub-categories Probability and Statistics were combined. The types of test items which focus on mathematical concepts are listed as are the skills related to the five main categories of content assessed in the written or practical tests.

## The practical tests (Chapter 2)

3 Practical skills were tested in eleven topics, including two new areas developed for this survey (Calculators and Length) and three new problem solving topics. The results for three of the topics (Area, Capacity/volume and Symmetry) are discussed in some detail and the range of strategies used by pupils and their difficulties are reported. Differences in the performance of girls and boys are examined.

## The written tests: sub-category scores and background variables (Chapter 3)

4 Performance on the written tests is considered against six background variables representing the characteristics of the schools in the sample — region of country, location (metropolitan or non-metropolitan), size of the age-group, pupil/teacher ratio, take up of free school meals and school locality/catchment area. This is the first survey at secondary level in which more detailed information has been collected about the nature of the locality from which pupils are drawn.

5 Differences in the performance of boys and girls are examined, and there is some comparison with the results of the 1980 primary survey. The report stresses that the use of more sensitive background variables would be required before firm conclusions could be drawn about the relationships between the background variables and levels of performance. More information is being collected on certain school characteristics and it is intended that the retrospective report on the initial five surveys will include fuller descriptions of mathematical performance and the factors affecting it.

## The written tests: item clusters (Chapter 4)

6 Responses given to clusters of test items reported in this chapter come from the sub-categories given greater emphasis in the 1980 survey — Geometry (Angles on a straight line and in triangles, Reflection and rotation), Number (Division and Powers and roots) and Measures (Area and perimeter). Variations in the context, presentation and complexity of these test items which influenced the levels of performance are discussed. Results are considered alongside analyses of the errors made and the omission and success rates, which provide a clearer picture of some of the factors affecting pupils' performance and an insight into the nature of pupils' understanding of these topics.

## Attitudes (Chapter 5)

7 A sub-sample of 1,140 pupils was asked to respond to a set of 36 statements expressing positive and negative opinions about mathematics and to rate a list of 17 mathematical topics and activities in terms of their perceived usefulness and interest. The questionnaire also incorporated a more specific attitude

measure consisting of a set of 17 items chosen from the written tests which pupils were asked to attempt before rating them in terms of difficulty, usefulness and interest.

8  The results show that about three-quarters of pupils considered mathematics to be important for a career and in everyday life. More girls than boys thought that mathematics was difficult, although, compared to girls, boys tended to over-estimate the ease of individual mathematical problems.

### Problems, applications, investigations: a review of development (Chapter 6)

9  This chapter describes the development of assessment instruments to test aspects of problem solving. An initial framework of six assessment categories was devised (processing information, formulating problems, strategies and methods of solution, generalising solutions, proving, evaluating results). These formed the basis for written tests which were piloted in the 1980 surveys, most of which related to the Generalisation and Strategies of solution categories. Practical test items were also developed and the results of one topic ('Tiles') are reported in considerable detail.

### The pattern of results: a review of three surveys (Chapter 7)

10  The pattern of performance in the 1980 survey was similar to that observed in the first two surveys. The differences in performance of 11 and 15 year old pupils on individual items were examined. Regional performance was highly consistent in nearly all the sub-categories over the three surveys. Pupils from the south of England achieved the highest mean scores in almost all the sub-categories whilst pupils from Wales tended to obtain the lowest, particularly in the more 'modern' sub-categories of modern algebra, modern geometry and probability and statistics. Performance between regions at age 15 is compared with that found at age 11 and some interesting contrasts appear; for instance, at age 11, pupils from Northern Ireland achieved the highest mean scores in almost all of the sub-categories and 11 year old pupils from Wales achieved the second highest scores in the more 'traditional' sub-categories.

11  In all three surveys the mean scores of boys were higher than girls on nearly every sub-category. Analyses show that these

differences in performance are greatest in the top 10 per cent attainment band where 62 per cent are boys and 38 per cent girls. However, in the lowest 10 per cent attainment band, the ratio of boys to girls is about equal. Performance scores were highest where the school was based in a non-metropolitan area, where fewer pupils took free school meals and where there were between 15 and 17 pupils per teacher.

12 Some patterns in the results over the three surveys are being investigated further. For example, investigations into differences in attainment between boys and girls on individual items and item clusters are to be carried out which should yield more information on these variations in performance.

# 1 The 1980 survey

## The 1980 survey

1.1 This report is an account of the results of the third survey in an initial series of five concerned with assessing the mathematics performance of pupils in schools in England, Wales and Northern Ireland. Pupils in the survey sample attained the age of 16 years during the year 1980–81.

1.2 The survey took place in November 1980 and was conducted by the National Foundation for Educational Research on behalf of the Assessment of Performance Unit at the Department of Education and Science. The work is sponsored by the DES, the Welsh Office and the Department of Education for Northern Ireland.

1.3 As in both previous surveys, written tests were administered to a representative national sample of pupils in the age group. Separate sub-samples of the main sample also completed either practical tests or attitude questionnaires. A further sub-sample of the main sample took pilot written tests concerned with problem solving. None of these tests was timed; schools were asked to give as much time as was practicable and as individual pupils appeared to need.

1.4 In 1980 the size of the main sample was 13,303 pupils of which 9,026 pupils were from schools in England, 2,258 from schools in Wales and 2,019 from schools in Northern Ireland. About 700 schools were involved in the survey.

[1] *Mathematical development. Secondary survey report No. 1.* HMSO, 1980, price £6.60

1.5 The sampling procedure was the same as for the surveys in 1978 and 1979 and has been fully described in Secondary Survey Report No. 1.[1] It is not designed to enable comparisons to be made between individual pupils, schools or Local Education Authorities, and consequently such comparisons cannot be validly made with the data obtained.

1.6 The Monitoring Services Unit at the NFER was responsible for contacting LEAs and schools in order to secure the sample and also for the supervision and organisation of the administrative arrangements for testing.

## The survey assessments

1.7 Each of the pupils in the sample was given one of 25 different written tests of mathematical concepts and skills. These tests contained short response items, many of which were included in the written tests given to all pupils in the 1978 and 1979 samples. About 150 new items were written for this survey, mostly in the sub-categories Number concepts, Unit measures and Descriptive geometry. This survey was the first in which a more detailed coverage of some areas was being made. In order to make room for the new items, this survey did not include as separate sub-categories Rate and ratio, Probability and Statistics as was the case in 1978 and 1979. Some items from Rate and ratio were included in Number applications and the Probability and Statistics sub-categories were combined.

1.8 In the practical mathematics survey 11 topics were assessed, several of which were new or amended from previous surveys. The tests were administered by experienced teachers of the age group who were nominated by their Local Education Authorities and trained to administer the tests by the NFER monitoring team. The tests were given to 1,140 pupils from the 228 schools in the practical survey sub-sample.

1.9 In the attitude questionnaire pupils were asked to respond to statements about their enjoyment of mathematics, how difficult they found it and how useful they thought it to be. They were also asked to attempt items representative of some mathematical topics and to indicate whether they found them interesting, difficult and useful. Up to six pupils from each of the 185 schools in the sub-sample responded to attitude questionnaires.

## The assessments and assessment framework: recent developments

**Problem solving strategies**

1.10 The main features of the assessment framework (Figure 1.1) are the same as those described in the first secondary survey report. However, the scheme is continually reviewed in the light of the results of successive surveys and as new assessment procedures are incorporated. In 1979, categories of context were added to the framework in order to place more stress on the cross-curricular aspects of the monitoring. This year, the column in the framework labelled "investigations and problem solving strategies" contains the initial assessment categories that were proposed during the development work which has been in progress since 1979. In the practical survey this year, three topics were concerned solely with problems in mathematical and everyday contexts. In addition, several of the more standard topics contained smaller scale problem situations. Written tests of problem solving strategies were also administered this year to a sub-sample of the pupils who took the survey written tests of concepts and skills. These have now been revised for inclusion in the 1981 survey. Both practical and written test modes present the problems in a structured form with questions on various aspects of the situation, leading the pupil progressively through familiarisation with the materials and task to the main ideas which are involved. The possibility of including exploratory investigations to provide pupils with opportunities for more creative work is currently under consideration.

**Attitudes**

1.11 Pupils taking the practical tests this year were rated by the testers on scales relating to their willingness to handle apparatus, and their confidence, anxiety about success, verbal fluency and persistence. These scales have been added to the diagram of the framework.

**Concepts and skills**

1.12 The main dimensions of the framework are content and learning outcome. There are 15 sub-categories of content, although, in order to make room for more detailed coverage in some areas, not all of these were assessed in the written tests used on this occasion.

**Figure 1.1** *Assessment framework*

MODE OF ASSESSMENT: Outcomes can be assessed in written or practical test forms.

| Content \ Outcome | Concepts and skills | | | Problem solving strategies | Attitudes |
|---|---|---|---|---|---|
| **Number** | Concepts | Skills | Applications of number | | |
| **Measures** | Unit | Rate and ratio | Mensuration | Processing information<br>Formulating problems<br>Strategies and methods of solution<br>Generalising solutions<br>Proving<br>Evaluating results | Liking, difficulty and utility of mathematics as a subject |
| **Algebra** | General algebra | Traditional algebra | Modern algebra | Graphical algebra | Investigations/Creativity: to be developed |
| **Geometry** | Descriptive geometry | Modern geometry | Trigonometry | | Enjoyment, utility and difficulty of specific mathematical topics in the curriculum |
| **Probability and Statistics** | Probability | Statistics | | | Attitudes to practical mathematics: willingness to handle apparatus; confidence; anxiety about success; verbal fluency; persistence |

CONTEXT: The content can be set in Mathematical, Everyday or Other subject contexts

1.13 Mean scores are computed for each of the sub-categories of content. For this purpose, each item testing concepts and skills is assigned to one sub-category only – that one in which its content is considered to be most adequately represented. However, since mathematical ideas are highly interrelated, the boundaries between sub-categories are not seen as impermeable. Consequently, in addition to sub-category mean scores, the results of individual items are reported within groups or clusters of items of related content which may come from more than one sub-category.

1.14 The first secondary survey report provided some definitions of 'concepts', 'skills' and also of another sub-category of learning outcome, 'applications'. Recently 'applications' have come to be seen as concepts and skills tested in various contexts, especially 'other subject' and 'everyday' contexts, and are no longer included as a separate outcome. Learning outcomes can be tested in either of the two modes of assessment: written or practical.

1.15 It was recognised that the categories of learning outcome are not clearly differentiated and also that the classification of an item must depend in part on the way in which a pupil tackles it. The implication is that an item cannot be regarded as testing purely a concept or a skill although it may focus more on one of these outcomes than on the other. It was partly due to these considerations that the idea emerged of deriving information from the results by contrasting the response patterns of several items in an item cluster rather than attempting to interpret the responses of isolated ones (see Chapter 4).

1.16 'Concept' refers to mathematical entities such as 'parallel', 'angle', 'prime number', 'square root', 'equation', 'average', 'number', 'proof'. Clearly these examples are not all at the same level of generality: the structure of mathematical knowledge can be seen as a network of linked concepts some of which are subordinate to others. Even the simplest concept has a large number of aspects and a particular item may test only one of them. For example, concepts can be represented verbally, in a diagram or in symbols and several items may be required to assess each of these aspects. Additional items may be needed to assess pupils' knowledge of a concept's attributes (classifying and identifying mathematical entities or noting similarities and differences between them) and their understanding of its relationship to other linked concepts.

1.17 The main types of concept are: (i) class concepts such as 'triangle', 'factors of 12', 'prime numbers', consisting of individual entities which can be sorted into groups labelled with the concept name; (ii) relations, which link two or more objects e.g. 'is parallel to', 'is longer than'; (iii) operations like 'multiplication', 'squaring', 'intersection' and 'enlarging', which are rules for changing the state of a mathematical entity; and (iv) notational concepts: the means by which mathematical relationships and ideas are represented. Notational concepts including 'place value', 'index', and ways of representing variables.

1.18 The following is a list of types of item which focus mainly on concepts and can appear in any content category but most of the examples given are from particular categories.

| Type | Examples |
|---|---|
| **(i) Representing concepts** | |
| Verbally | Supplying a definition |
| | Supplying an examplar given a definition |
| | Explaining and describing mathematical ideas and information |
| Visually | Representing fractions pictorially |
| Symbolically | Knowledge and understanding of conventions such as $\sqrt{\ }$; $x^2 + y$ |
| | Knowledge and understanding of notation e.g. stating the value of 2 in 5.32 |
| **(ii) Knowledge of concept's attributes** | |
| Sorting | Sorting shapes into categories |
| Identifying | Identifying prime numbers |
| Naming | Supplying the names of 3D shapes |
| **(iii) Relating concepts** | Relationship between $\times$ and $+$; area and perimeter; place value and decimals |
| **(iv) Comparing quantities** | |
| Applying a unit | Counting the number of equilateral triangles covering a shape |
| | Comparing the quantity of different sizes of units that can be applied to a given measurable entity e.g. how many inches/metres/paperclips in a desk length |
| | Finding the number of halves in $2\frac{1}{2}$ |
| Ordering quantities | Placing fractions/decimals in order of size |
| | Placing measures (e.g. areas) in order of size. |

1.19 The examples given in the list show that different levels of understanding of a concept can be tapped by an item, from simply remembering a definition to understanding how different aspects of a concept are related and how one concept is related to others.

1.20 Ultimately, the understanding of mathematical concepts is a matter of the way in which learners organise knowledge so that it is readily and flexibly available for use in appropriate situations. The availability cannot be properly demonstrated without involving skills.

1.21 'Skills' were defined in the first secondary survey report as learned routines, such as measuring with a ruler, using a subtraction algorithm, drawing a circle with compasses. However, just as the availability of concepts cannot be demonstrated without exercising skills, many skills or practised routines are dependent for their success on an understanding of underlying concepts. Moreover, as learning proceeds, the range of situations in which a practised skill can be used is widened and the range of procedures which become practised skills is also increased. Consequently the list of skills given below includes some which are at a higher level that the basic kinds, like using a ruler and calculating with algorithms, and might better be described as learned strategies than as learned routines. Skills can be related to the five main categories of content as listed below, but it is not supposed that each of the skills given will be confined to items in the related main category (i.e. that calculating skills will only be relevant to the Number sub-categories or visualising to the Geometry sub-categories). Higher level skills such as 'proving' appear in the list of problem solving strategies (see Figure 1.1).

| (i) Numerical | : | **Calculating**<br>Using calculating aids<br>Using algorithms<br>Approximating<br>Checking results |
|---|---|---|
| (ii) Measurement | : | **Measuring**<br>Using measuring instruments<br>Estimating |
| (iii) Algebraic | : | **Communicating information with symbols**<br>Expressing numerical, logical and geo-metrical relationships symbolically<br>Manipulating symbols: factorising, simplifying, using formulas |
| (iv) Statistical | : | **Communicating information about data**<br>Gathering data<br>Summarising data<br>Constructing, reading and interpreting charts, tables and graphs |
| (v) Geometrical | : | **Communicating spatial information**<br>Constructing, reading and interpreting scale drawings, models, diagrams<br>Using geometrical instruments<br>Visualising spatial relationships. |

1.22   Both concepts and skills can be assessed in either of the two modes used in the surveys: written or practical. In the practical there is an emphasis on communicating mathematical ideas and information and measurement in everyday contexts.

## Features of the report

1.23   The general pattern of the results is basically the same as in 1978 and 1979 and the policy of adding more detail to the general picture, rather than repeating what has been reported before, has been continued.

1.24   In Chapter 2, which is concerned with the results of the practical tests, detailed accounts are given of topics from the main content categories Measures (Area, Capacity/volume) and Geometry (Symmetry).

[1]Department of Education and Science (1979). *Aspects of secondary education in England*. HMSO.

1.25    Chapter 3 is concerned with written test sub-category scores in relation to background variables. It includes coverage of a new school catchment area variable derived from the HMI Secondary Survey[1] which provides a more detailed classification than the one used hitherto which describes LEAs as either metropolitan or non-metropolitan. This latter classification is an official designation which can be misleading; for example, all Authorities in Wales are designated as non-metropolitan although some contain highly urbanised areas.

1.26    Chapter 4 is an account of the responses given to clusters of items of related content in the written tests of concepts and skills from the content categories Geometry (Angles on a straight line and in triangles, Reflection and rotation), Number (Division and Powers and roots) and Measures (Area and perimeter). Differences between the items in a cluster are associated with corresponding variations in the patterns of responses made to them.

1.27    Chapter 5 discusses the 1980 findings on pupils' attitudes to mathematics. The attitudes of this age group were assessed for the first time in 1979 and, as on that occasion, the questionnaire contained scales measuring aspects of attitude to mathematics and a list of mathematical topics and activities to be rated by pupils. It also, again, contained a more specific attitude measure in which items from the written test of concepts and skills were presented to the pupils for working out before rating.

1.28    Chapter 6 is a report on the development of assessment instruments to test aspects of problem solving. This work stems from the feasibility study which was conducted at the NFER before the present project was established in 1977 and also from a conference of teachers and researchers held by the APU in 1979. Exploratory topics in the area have been employed in the primary practical assessments from the first survey but this year the first full scale piloting of written tests at both age levels took place. Revised versions of these have been included in the 1981 surveys.

1.29    The concluding Chapter 7 focuses on some of the particularly consistent features of the three surveys so far conducted. These relate mainly to the pattern of results against school variables but also includes differences between boys and girls.

# 2 The practical tests

## The practical tests

2.1   As in 1978 and 1979, the survey included the practical mode of assessment. The major change in the 1980 survey was the development of topics assessing problem solving skills. Two of these, Dominoes and Tiles, were concerned with number patterns and generalisations. Another, Journey to France, was a multi-stage problem set in an 'everyday' context. In addition, several of the more conventional topics were modified by the inclusion of problem solving questions. The progress made on developing problem solving assessment materials is discussed in Chapter 6.

2.2   Table 2.1 lists the eleven topics used in the survey. As well as the problem solving topics described above, Calculators and Length were also new topics developed for the 1980 survey. The Mass and Probability topics were considerably revised from the 1979 versions while the remaining four topics received only minor changes from the previous year's survey. Most of these changes resulted from the helpful comments and advice received from the testers who took part in the 1979 survey. They attended a half day meeting after the survey to discuss their experiences and, in addition, some of them undertook to try out revised versions of scripts in their schools.

## The design of the practical survey

2.3   The pupils selected for the practical assessment were a sub-sample of those taking the written concepts and skills tests. The practical survey took place between 7 November and 18 November. These dates were chosen so that approximately half the pupils took the written test before the practical and the remaining pupils took the practical test first.

**Table 2.1**  *Practical topics used in the 1980 secondary survey*

| Main content category | Practical topic and assessment objectives |
|---|---|
| **Number** | *Calculators* |
| | 1  Use of calculator |
| | 2  Making approximations |
| | 3  Checking calculations by inverse operations |
| | 4  Awareness of the importance of order of operations |
| | 5  Solving two stage problems |

| **Geometry** | *Angles* |
|---|---|
| | 1 Estimating right, acute, obtuse and reflex angles |
| | 2 Drawing acute and obtuse angles without a protractor |
| | 3 Measuring acute, obtuse and reflex angles |
| | 4 Estimating angles of a triangle |

*Symmetry*

1 Understanding of the construction of symmetrical patterns by folding paper
2 Understanding of the properties of lines of symmetry using a mirror
3 Use of properties of a line of symmetry to construct a pattern

**Measures**      *Area*

1 Comparing areas of 3- and 4-sided shapes
2 Measuring the area of a rectangle using a square unit
3 Estimating and measuring the area of an irregular shape

*Capacity/volume*

1 Estimating and checking the capacity of a rectangular box given a unit cube
2 Use of two different sizes and types of unit to measure capacity

*Length*

1 Estimating the lengths of straight and curved lines
2 Use of a ruler
3 Knowledge of appropriate means of measuring curved lines
4 Use of a scale

*Mass*

1 Understanding of the idea of a balance
2 Application of this idea to problems

**Probability and statistics**      *Probability*

1 Understanding of some aspects of the concept of probability
2 Methods of recording the outcomes of a series of chance events

**Problem solving**

*Dominoes*

1  Understanding of a set of rules of a game, performance in using rules to make highest-scoring moves
2  Understanding of a strategy for generating sequences of numbers
3  Recognition of a relationship between sequences of numbers
4  Ability to continue sequences of numbers

*Journey to France*

1  Use of charts and map
2  Solution of a multi-stage problem

*Tiles*

1  Recognition of patterns and relationships
2  Continuing patterns and hypothesising generalisations

2.4  Each pupil was given a practical test consisting of two or three topics chosen from the list in Table 2.1. The problem solving topics (Dominoes, Journey to France, Tiles) generally took longer than the more conventional topics because of their exploratory nature. Therefore, tests either consisted of one problem solving topic with one other topic or three of the more traditional topics. Table 2.2 shows the combinations of topics used in each test.

**Table 2.2**  *Test design: topics in each test*

| TEST | TOPIC 1 | TOPIC 2 | TOPIC 3 |
|------|---------|---------|---------|
| 1 | Tiles | Angles | — |
| 2 | Area | Tiles | — |
| 3 | Journey to France | Mass | — |
| 4 | Symmetry | Journey to France | — |
| 5 | Dominoes | Probability | — |
| 6 | Capacity/volume | Dominoes | — |
| 7 | Length | Calculators | Capacity/volume |
| 8 | Angles | Mass | Probability |
| 9 | Symmetry | Capacity/volume | Area |
| 10 | Probability | Length | Calculators |
| 11 | Mass | Angles | Length |
| 12 | Calculators | Area | Symmetry |

2.5  The tests were administered by 31 experienced teachers of the survey age group nominated by their Local Education Authorities. They were trained at a 3-day residential conference held in September 1980. At the conference, testers were shown videotapes of each topic and practised filling in the scripts by taking part in simulated interviews. After the conference, testers administered the topics to pupils in their own schools in order to gain further experience. Their completed scripts were checked by monitoring team members and comments sent back so as to improve the consistency of test administration.

2.6   Testers visited up to eight schools each and tested five pupils in each school. In total, 1140 pupils were tested in 228 schools. Every tester received instructions on which tests to use for each day of the survey, the combinations of tests being chosen so that every topic was given at least once in each school and only one topic was given twice. Thus, any effects that might have arisen due to exposure of a topic within a school were controlled. In addition, the order in which the tests were administered on each day was designed to balance any effects due to the order in which pupils came for testing. For example, schools might arrange for boys to be tested in the morning and girls in the afternoon and, if the tests were given in a fixed order on each day, then this would result in unbalanced samples of boys and girls taking each topic.

2.7   The layout of the topic scripts used by testers was similar to that employed in the 1979 survey (see second secondary mathematics report). Below is an extract from the script of the Area topic.

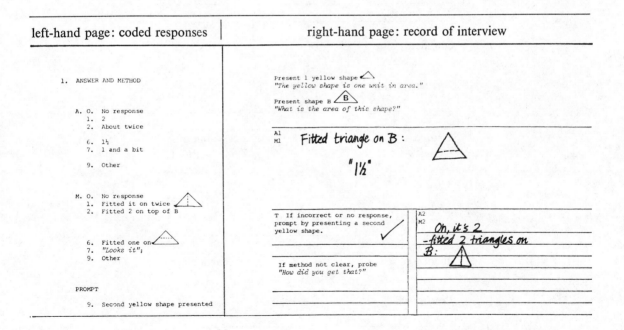

2.8   Testers recorded the interview on the right-hand pages. Instructions to testers are printed in ordinary type and the actual words spoken by the testers are printed in italics. Opposite each question a list of coded responses was given; those marked with an asterisk were considered to be acceptable responses. The codes provided guidance on the likely responses, but after the survey these were amended in the light of pupils' performance.

2.9   In the example given above, the pupil's initial answer and method are recorded in the plain section below the question. Since the response was incorrect, the tester gave the prompt listed in the script and the pupil's subsequent answer and method are recorded on the lined section. For many questions, recommended prompts were included in the script and testers were asked to use only those, unless particular circumstances merited additional prompts being given.

2.10   One development for the 1980 survey was that testers were asked to assess pupils' approach to topics under five headings. For each category, testers were required to rate the pupils on a five point scale as indicated below.

*Willingness to handle apparatus*

| | | | | |
|---|---|---|---|---|

very
willing

very
reluctant

*Confidence*

| | | | | |
|---|---|---|---|---|

over
confident

shy,
reserved

*Attitude to test*

| | | | | |
|---|---|---|---|---|

assured

anxious
about
success

*Ability to express explanations*

| | | | | |
|---|---|---|---|---|

fluent

inarticulate

*Persistence*

| | | | | |
|---|---|---|---|---|

very
persistent

gives up
easily

2.11   This was the first occasion that such an assessment was attempted and the results should be treated with caution since it was only viewed as a pilot study.

## Results of selected topics

2.12   The results of three of the topics (Area, Capacity/volume and Symmetry) used in the 1980 survey are reported here. In addition, the Tiles topic is discussed in Chapter 6 (Problems, applications and investigations).

2.13   For each topic, the questions are reproduced from the script used by testers. After each question there is a table of results showing separately for boys and girls the percentages giving certain responses. In all cases these are the responses given by pupils before any intervention on the part of the tester. Acceptable responses are denoted by an asterisk.

2.14   One consequence of using different combinations of tests each day was that there were different sample sizes for some topics. Four topics (Calculators, Capacity/volume, Length and Probability) had sample sizes of around 270–280 pupils, while the other topics were each given to between 220 and 230 pupils. The number of pupils who took each of the topics discussed in this chapter is:

| Area | 221 |
| Capacity/volume | 272 |
| Symmetry | 224 |

2.15   The relatively small sample size for the practical topics needs to be borne in mind when interpreting the results. The confidence limits for the data reported here can be as high as $\pm$ 7 per cent. In other words, there are 95 chances out of 100 that, for any particular question, the mean of the population as a whole lies somewhere in a band with an upper limit of 7 per cent above the reported score and a lower limit 7 per cent below it.

2.16   For some questions, the differences between boys' and girls' results are indicated as being significant: this refers to statistical significance at the 5 per cent level. The meaning of such differences is discussed in Appendix 2.

**Area**

2.17   This topic assessed pupils' performance in comparing the areas of 3- and 4-sided shapes and in measuring the area of a rectangle given a square unit. Pupils were also asked to estimate and then measure the area of an irregular shape.

2.18   First, pupils were asked to find the area of two shapes using a triangle as the unit of area. Question 1 is shown below.

---

1.   Present 1 yellow shape
     *"The yellow shape is one unit in area."*

     Present shape B
     *"What is the area of this shape?"*

---

2.19  It should be noted that the shapes are not reproduced to size. The correct answer is 2 units which can be demonstrated by placing the unit triangle on triangle B as indicated below.

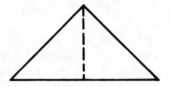

2.20  Some pupils placed the unit triangle on triangle B in one of the ways shown below and then estimated the area.

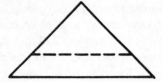

2.21  Other pupils made a visual estimate of the area without handling the shapes. The full results are given below.

Results of question 1 (*figures in italics are percentages*).

| Answer \ Method | Fitted Triangle on 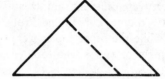 * | Visual Estimate | Fitted Triangle on  | Other Method | Method not Recorded | Total |
|---|---|---|---|---|---|---|
| *  2 | 23 | 26 | 12 | 3 | 6 | 70 |
| 1½ or other fraction between 1 & 2 | — | 1 | 12 | 3 | 3 | 19 |
| Other | — | — | 1 | 1 | 4 | 6 |
| Total | 23 | 27 | 25 | 7 | 13 | 95 |
| | | | | | No response | 5 |

2.22  The table shows that a range of methods was chosen by the 70 per cent of pupils (72 per cent boys, 68 per cent girls) who gave the correct response of 2 units for the area. Almost all pupils who made a visual estimate of the area gave the correct answer, whereas only about half of those who fitted the unit triangle onto shape B in one of the ways which required an estimate were correct.

2.23  Unsuccessful pupils were presented with a second yellow triangle as an aid in comparing the shapes. After this, a further 24 per cent obtained the correct answer.

2.24  In the next question pupils were asked for the area of a parallelogram, using the same triangle as the unit of area.

---

2.  Present shape D

"*What is the area of this shape?*"

---

2.25  The correct answer is 4 units which can be demonstrated by fitting either the unit triangle or triangle B onto the parallelogram as shown below.

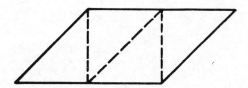   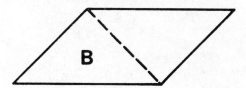

Results of question 2 (*figures in italics are percentages*)

| Method \ Answer | Fitted Triangle on * | Fitted Triangle B on * | Visual Estimate | Other Method | Method not Recorded | Total |
|---|---|---|---|---|---|---|
| * 4 | 29 | 29 | 6 | 9 | 2 | 75 |
| 3 | — | — | 3 | 5 | 3 | 11 |
| Other | — | — | 2 | 4 | 3 | 9 |
| Total | 29 | 29 | 11 | 18 | 8 | 95 |
| | | | | | No response | 5 |

2.26  With the parallelogram, the proportion of pupils making a visual estimate of the area dropped by over half compared with triangle B, possibly because the shape was larger and so pupils had less confidence in their ability to judge visually.

2.27   The difference in success rates for boys and girls was reversed on question 2, with 73 per cent of the boys and 77 per cent of the girls giving the correct response.

2.28   The next question also involved comparison of area:

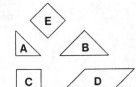

3.   Present shapes A, B, C, D.
Present shape E (blue) as diamond.
*"Which of shapes A, B, C, D are equal in area to this shape E. You can pick the shapes up if you like."*

| Answers | Boys | Girls | Total |
|---|---|---|---|
| | % | % | % |
| * B and C | 31 | 20 | 26 |
| C only | 61 | 69 | 65 |
| B and/or C with incorrect shape(s) | 6 | 7 | 6 |
| Other | 2 | 2 | 2 |
| No response | 0 | 2 | 1 |

2.29   Most pupils readily identified C as being equal in area to shape E. Those pupils who gave only shape C as their response were asked if there were any others equal in area to E and after this, a further 29 per cent correctly identified shape B. Various methods were used to discover that B and E were equal; about half the pupils compared each with the unit triangle A, while others compared B and E directly, usually in one of the ways illustrated in Figure 2.1 below:

**Figure 2.1**   *Comparing shapes B and E.*

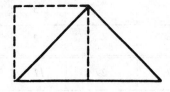
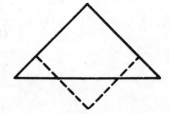

2.30   Those pupils who used one of the methods shown in Figure 2.1 estimated that the overlapping portions of B and E compensated for each other.

2.31   For the next task, pupils were asked to find the area of a rectangle using a square tile as one unit.

4.   Present plastic tile.
   *"Now take this square to be one unit in area."*
   Present sheet with rectangle AR(1)
   *"What is the area of this shape in these units?"*

Figure 2.2 below shows how the tile fitted onto the rectangle.

**Figure 2.2**   *Area of rectangle AR(1)*

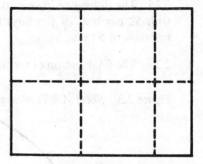

2.32   Some pupils used the tile to find the length and width of the rectangle and then multiplied them together to get their answer. Others fitted the tile onto the rectangle four times and then estimated the remaining portion. The full results are given below.

Results of question 4 ( *figures in italics are percentages*).

| Answer \ Method | Length × width * | 4 whole, estimated rest | Visual estimate | Other | Total |
|---|---|---|---|---|---|
| *   5 | 18 | 30 | — | 2 | 50 |
| 4 | — | — | 2 | 6 | 8 |
| 6 | 14 | — | 2 | 8 | 24 |
| 4 – 5 | 1 | 5 | — | — | 6 |
| Other | 3 | 2 | 2 | 4 | 11 |
| Total | 36 | 37 | 6 | 20 | 99 |
| No response | | | | | 1 |

2.33   It is interesting to note that half the pupils who chose the 'length × width' rule to find the area gave the wrong answer. This was often due to careless placement of the tile on the rectangle.

2.34   There was a further decline in the proportion of pupils making a visual estimate on this question; 6 per cent adopted this method compared with 11 per cent for the parallelogram and 27 per cent for triangle B. This is probably due to the size of the rectangle. In fact, no-one gave a correct visual estimate for the area. However, those pupils who found that the tile fitted onto the rectangle 4 times and then estimated the remaining portion generally obtained the correct answer.

2.35   The difference in success rates between boys and girls was not significant with 52 per cent of the boys and 47 per cent of the girls giving the correct response of 5 units.

2.36   The final section of the topic concerned an irregular shape (see figure 2.3).

**Figure 2.3**   *Sheet AR(2) presented to pupils*

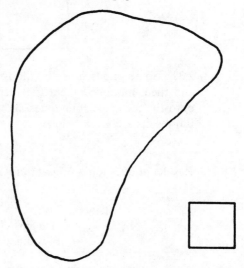

---

5.   Present plain sheet with irregular shape AR(2).
"*Still using this square as 1 unit in area* (demonstrate that the tile fits on the square), *make a rough estimate of the area of this shape.*"

---

The purpose of the question was to seek a visual comparison of the shapes on sheet AR(2). It should be noted that the tile was not available for pupils to experiment with.

2.37   The actual answer was between 15 and 16 units and answers between 10 and 20 inclusive were considered acceptable. These limits were decided after discussion with testers.

Results of question 5

| Answers | Boys % | Girls % | Total % |
|---|---|---|---|
| * $10 \leqslant$ area $\leqslant 14$ | 28 | 24 | 26 |
| * $14 <$ area $< 17$ | 17 | 23 | 20 |
| * $17 \leqslant$ area $\leqslant 20$ | 25 | 25 | 25 |
| Total acceptable | 70 | 72 | 71 |
| $< 10$ | 3 | 5 | 3 |
| $> 20$ | 22 | 15 | 19 |
| Other | 4 | 3 | 4 |
| No response | 1 | 3 | 2 |
| Question not put | 0 | 2 | 1 |

2.38   Next, pupils were asked for a more accurate method of determining the area of the irregular shape.

---

6.   *"Can you think of a method for getting a more accurate estimate of the area?"*

---

| Answers | Boys % | Girls % | Total % |
|---|---|---|---|
| *Use a grid, squared paper or graph paper | 47 | 30 | 39 |
| *Draw round tile | 3 | 5 | 4 |
| Put string round perimeter then make into rectangle | 4 | 11 | 7 |
| Draw a rectangle round it | 4 | 2 | 3 |
| Other | 28 | 27 | 28 |
| No response | 14 | 22 | 18 |
| Question not put | 0 | 3 | 1 |

2.39   It is interesting to note that 7 per cent of the pupils believed that shapes with equal perimeter would have equal area. They suggested placing string around the outside of the shape in order to determine the perimeter, then arranging the string as a rectangle and calculating the area as length × width.

2.40   Regardless of their responses to the above question, pupils were presented with a diagram of the same shape drawn on a grid (see Figure 2.4).

**Figure 2.4**   *Sheet AR(3) presented to pupils*

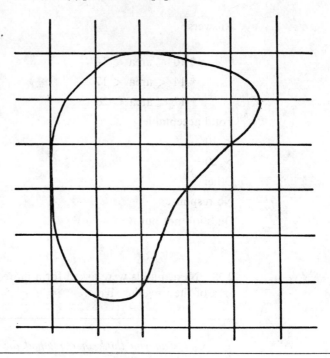

7.   Present irregular shape on grid AR(3).

"*Here is the same shape drawn on a grid with squares the same size as this.* (Demonstrate).
*Find the area of the shape. You may mark the paper.*"

| Answers | Boys % | Girls % | Total % |
|---|---|---|---|
| *$14\frac{1}{2}$ – $16\frac{1}{2}$ incl. | 51 | 53 | 52 |
| < $14\frac{1}{2}$ | 33 | 27 | 30 |
| > $16\frac{1}{2}$ | 12 | 9 | 11 |
| Other | 2 | 0 | 1 |
| No response | 2 | 8 | 5 |
| Question not put | 0 | 3 | 1 |

2.41   When asked how they got their answer, over 80 per cent of pupils said they had counted the whole squares and then attempted to match up the part squares to make whole ones. A few pupils had chosen to count only parts greater than a half square and ignore others.

2.42   Testers generally considered the topic straightforward and appropriate to the age group. Some commented that pupils were unfamiliar with using a triangle as a unit of area and that greater confidence was apparent when using a square unit.

*Comparison between boys and girls*

2.43 Two questions produced significantly different success rates for boys and girls. On question 3, concerning which of shapes A–D were equal in area to shape E, 31 per cent of the boys gave both correct answers compared with 20 per cent of the girls. Question 6, asking for methods of obtaining a more accurate estimate of the area of the irregular shape, also produced significantly different results for boys and girls, with 50 per cent of the boys suggesting suitable ways compared with 35 per cent of the girls. Other questions on the Area topic do not show any pattern of differences between boys and girls.

2.44 The rating of pupils' approaches to the topic reveal some differences between the sexes (see Figure 2.5).

**Figure 2.5** *Area topic: Testers' ratings of pupils*

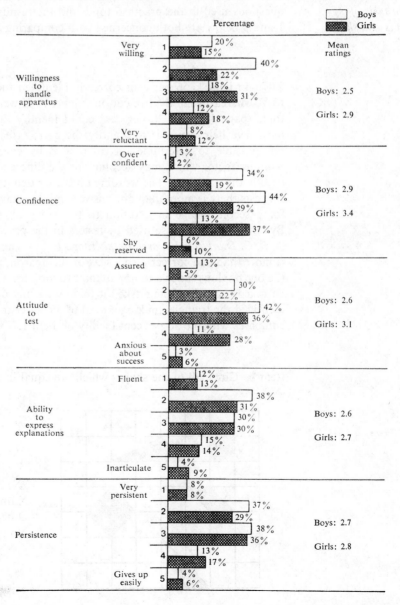

2.45   The results show large differences between the sexes on the scales assessing confidence and attitude to the topic. Boys tended to be rated as confident and assured whereas girls tended to be more reserved and showed anxiety about their performance. Another feature of the results is that boys were assessed as more willing to handle the apparatus than girls. This may account for the lower success rate for girls on the question involving comparison of shapes A–E. Similar assessments for boys and girls were made on the scales assessing persistence and ability to express explanations.

*Comparison with written tests of concepts and skills*

2.46   Some items from the Unit measures sub-category are similar to some questions used in the practical topic and the results are compared here. Items 1 and 2 below are both concerned with comparing areas drawn on a grid.

2.47   In item 1, 56 per cent correctly identified the two shapes equal in area to V, whereas when the five cut-out shapes A–E were presented in the practical topic (page 16) only 26 per cent could identify the correct shapes. The grid may have helped pupils to identify the correct shapes in item 1, though it is not possible to determine the area of Z by counting triangles or squares. Another factor which may account for the difference in facility is the wording used in the questions. The wording on the written item "*circle all of the shapes*" suggests there is more than one answer and this may encourage pupils to search for a second shape in addition to the fairly obvious response of shape X. By contrast, the phrase used by testers in the practical topic "*which of shapes A, B, C, D are equal in area to this shape E*" does not make it so clear that there is more than one correct response. For this reason, pupils may be satisfied with the one obvious shape and not attempt to look for additional answers. It should be noted that after being asked if there were any others, a further 29 per cent identified the triangle, making a total of 55 per cent with the full answer, which compares with the 56 per cent facility on item 1.

**Item 1**   Circle all of the shapes which are equal in area to shape V.

| Response | % |
|---|---|
| *X, Z | 56 |
| X only | 20 |
| Other | 17 |
| No response | 7 |

**Item 2**   Which shape is not equal in area to the other five?

| Response | % |
|---|---|
| G | 10 |
| H | 1 |
| J | 1 |
| K | 10 |
| L | 9 |
| *M | 67 |
| No response | 2 |

2.48   Item 2 also involves comparison of area and it is interesting to note that, while 67 per cent correctly selected M, the most common errors were to select G, K or L. A possible explanation for these choices is that they look quite different from any of the others. Shape G fills one of the squares of the grid whereas all the other shapes overlap two or more squares. The elongated triangle K and the concave shape L may be chosen because they have thin sections which are thought by some pupils to have a smaller area.

2.49   Item 3 below asks for an estimation of an irregular area. The actual answer is around 7000 km² and responses between 5000 and 9000 were coded as correct. This margin is roughly equivalent to that allowed on the question in the practical topic asking for an estimation of an irregular area, yet 10 per cent gave acceptable answers in the written test compared with 71 per cent in the practical.

**Item 3**

Use your judgement to find an estimate of the area of the shaded part of the island, a map of which is shown below. The island measures approximately 200 km from top to bottom and the horizontal and vertical scales are the same.

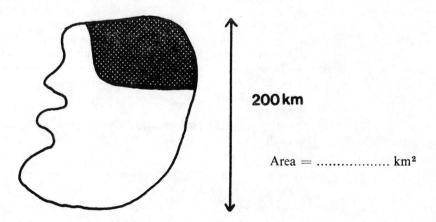

200 km

Area = ................. km²

2.50   The written test item was complicated by the use of a scale. Some pupils may have thought that the shaded part was half to a quarter as large as the whole and found that fraction of 200 km, rather than using the area. 22 per cent of pupils gave responses in the range 50 – 90 km² and these results could have been obtained in this way.

2.51   Other pupils may have attempted to estimate the area of the whole island rather than just the shaded part. Another difference between the written and practical test items is that the practical question used a square as the unit of area and pupils may have found it easier to picture how many times the square would fit into the shape. Also, pupils had already used the square unit to find the area of a rectangle and thus had some idea of what size answer would seem reasonable.

2.52   Other results on area questions from the written concepts and skills tests are discussed in Chapter 4, paragraphs 4.20 to 4.34.

**Capacity/volume**   2.53   This topic assessed pupils' performance in using different sizes and types of units to measure the volumes of a cuboid and a cylinder.

2.54   First, pupils were required to make a visual estimate of how many cubes would fit into a perspex box.

---

1.   Present large perspex box, hold one wooden cube in hand (do not give to pupil).
   *"Estimate how many of these cubes will fill this box."*

---

2.55   The actual dimensions of the box, in terms of the length of side of the cube, were $5 \times 4 \times 3$, meaning that 60 cubes would fit in. Estimates between 36 and 90 inclusive were considered acceptable. Pupils were asked how they had obtained their answer and a majority indicated that they had estimated the three dimensions of the box and then multiplied them together. The full results are given below.

Results of question 1 (*all figures in italics are percentages*)

| Answer \ Method | *Length × width × height | *Base area × height or equivalent | Guess | Other | Total |
|---|---|---|---|---|---|
| < 36 | 5 | — | 3 | 9 | 17 |
| *36 ≤ estimate < 60 | 17 | 1 | 4 | 6 | 28 |
| *60 | 21 | 1 | — | 2 | 24 |
| *60 < estimate ≤ 90 | 11 | 1 | — | 2 | 14 |
| < 90 | 10 | — | 1 | 5 | 16 |
| Other | — | — | — | 1 | 1 |
| Total | 64 | 3 | 8 | 25 | 100 |

2.56   The methods chosen to tackle this question were similar for boys and girls, but there were some differences between sexes in the answers obtained. 29 per cent of boys and 21 per cent of girls gave the exact response of 60, while 22 per cent of boys and 33 per cent of girls gave estimates in the range 36 to 60. Pupils were then presented with some cubes and asked to check their estimate. They were given more than 60 cubes in case they wanted to fill the box, but an attempt was made, if they started to do this, to direct them to a method such as length × width × height.

---

2.   Present cubes.

"*Check your estimate. You don't have to use all of the cubes*".

---

| Answers | Boys % | Girls % | Total % |
|---|---|---|---|
| * 60, length × width × height | 61 | 52 | 56 |
| * 60, 1 layer × height | 14 | 16 | 15 |
| Attempts to fill box | 16 | 18 | 17 |
| Other | 9 | 14 | 12 |

2.57   Those pupils who appeared to be filling the box were prompted towards using a more efficient method:—

---

Prompt   If after one layer, pupil appears to be filling box repeat

"*You don't have to use all of the cubes*".

---

2.58   Other pupils had merely made an arithmetical error in their calculation and were told to check their answer. After these prompts, all but 6 per cent of the pupils obtained the correct answer of 60. Since this question was essential to the rest of the topic, testers demonstrated the answer for unsuccessful pupils by filling the bottom layer with 20 cubes and showing how 3 layers would fit in.

2.59   The next section of the topic involved measuring the volume of the same box with spheres instead of cubes and then establishing the relationship between the two units.

---

3.   Present small box.

"*This small box will hold one cube.*" (Demonstrate)

Present bag of spheres.

"*How would you use the small box to find about how many of these spheres fill the big box?*"

---

2.60   Since it had been established that the big box held 60 cubes, the problem could be solved simply by seeing how many spheres filled the small box and then multiplying the answer by 60.

| Answers | Boys | Girls | Total |
|---|---|---|---|
| | % | % | % |
| * Count how many spheres fill small box, × by 60 | 77 | 82 | 79 |
| Other | 20 | 17 | 19 |
| No response | 3 | 1 | 2 |

Of those who made no response or were incorrect, about half were told the necessary procedure by testers and the remainder were able to describe the correct method after prompting.

2.61   Pupils were then asked to carry out the task they had just explained, or had been told, in order to determine roughly how many spheres would fill the big box.

---

4.   *"Do it."*

---

2.62   Depending on how the spheres were packed, it was possible to fit 6, 7 or 8 of them into the small box, thus giving answers of 360, 420 or 480 respectively for the number of spheres that would fill the big box.

| Answers | Boys | Girls | Total |
|---|---|---|---|
| | % | % | % |
| * 360 | 30 | 27 | 28 |
| * 420 | 18 | 12 | 15 |
| * 480 | 27 | 33 | 30 |
| Other | 23 | 27 | 25 |
| No response | 2 | 1 | 2 |

2.63   Most errors were due to faulty arithmetic rather than to an incorrect procedure. All pupils had got as far as discovering how many spheres filled the small box and so were asked the next question.

---

5.   Show one cube and one sphere.

*"If we say this cube is one unit of volume, what can you say about the volume of a sphere?"*

---

| Answers | Boys | Girls | Total |
|---|---|---|---|
| | % | % | % |
| * $\frac{1}{6}$, $\frac{1}{7}$ or $\frac{1}{8}$ | 70 | 59 | 64 |
| 6, 7 or 8 times smaller | 1 | 1 | 1 |
| 0.6, 0.7 or 0.8 | 0 | 3 | 2 |
| Other | 17 | 17 | 17 |
| No response | 12 | 20 | 16 |

2.64   Those pupils who could not give the relationship between the volume of a cube and the volume of a sphere were prompted:

---

Prompt   *"How many spheres make one unit of volume?"*

---

2.65   After this, a further 8 per cent were able to give the correct fraction for the volume of a sphere. The next question was put only to those who had succeeded in stating the relationship between the two units of volume.

---

6.   *"Is that exact, or is the volume of a sphere more than* .....................
*or less than* .....................*?"*

---

| Answers | Boys | Girls | Total |
|---|---|---|---|
| | % | % | % |
| * Less than | 58 | 46 | 52 |
| More than | 16 | 20 | 18 |
| Exact | 5 | 7 | 6 |
| Other | 1 | 1 | 1 |
| Question not put | 20 | 26 | 23 |

2.66   Most pupils appreciated that the volume of a sphere could not be given exactly because the spheres did not completely fill the small box but left gaps. However, some pupils interpreted this as meaning that the true volume of a sphere would be more than the fraction they had given earlier. Examples of this reasoning are shown below.

*"More because there's space left over so if the spheres fitted in better there would be more of them".*
*"More because the spheres don't fit together".*

2.67   The final section of the topic was concerned with finding the volume of an open-topped cylindrical tin. Pupils were first asked to suggest a suitable method using any of the items at their disposal: the large box, small box, cubes and spheres.

7.   Present tin.
"*Using the apparatus here, how would you find the approximate volume of this tin?*"

| Answers | Boys % | Girls % | Total % |
|---|---|---|---|
| * Fill tin with spheres, count, then ÷ by 6, 7 or 8 | 31 | 31 | 31 |
| * Fill with cubes and spheres and necessary calculation | 6 | 2 | 4 |
| * Fill in groups of 6, 7 or 8, count groups | 10 | 7 | 9 |
| * Other correct | 4 | 1 | 2 |
| Fill with spheres, no further | 17 | 24 | 21 |
| Fill with cubes, no further | 2 | 4 | 3 |
| Fill with cubes and spheres, no further | 6 | 3 | 4 |
| Other incorrect | 17 | 17 | 17 |
| No response | 7 | 11 | 9 |

2.68   After prompting, a further 9 per cent described a suitable method for finding the volume of the tin and 28 per cent were told how to do it:

If incorrect or no response, explain
"*Fill the tin with spheres, divide by 6, 7, 8 because you found that 6, 7, 8 spheres made 1 unit of volume.*"

2.69   Thus, a total of 83 per cent of pupils had either described or been told an appropriate procedure for finding the volume of the tin. Most of the remaining pupils had described in part a suitable method and so all but 2 per cent of the sample were asked to carry out the task of finding the volume of the tin.

8.   "*Do so*".

Results of question 8 (*all figures in italics are percentages*)

| Method / Answer | Filled with spheres, ÷ 6, 7 or 8 * | Filled with cubes and spheres and necessary calculation * | Filled in groups of 6, 7 or 8 count groups * | Filled bottom of tin, × by height ÷ by 6, 7 or 8 * | Filled with spheres only | Other incorrect | Total |
|---|---|---|---|---|---|---|---|
| *54–60 spheres (or equivalent) correct calculation | 32 | 2 | 9 | 6 | — | — | 49 |
| 54–60 spheres (or equivalent) incorrect calculation | 4 | — | — | 1 | — | — | 5 |
| Other | 16 | 5 | 3 | 1 | 12 | 5 | 42 |
| Total | 52 | 7 | 12 | 8 | 12 | 5 | 96 |

| | |
|---|---|
| No response | 2 |
| Question not put | 2 |

2.70   The tin held between 54 and 60 spheres inclusive depending on how they were packed. Pupils who either put less than 54 spheres into the tin or piled the spheres up above the rim are classified under "other answers". The table of results shows that 79 per cent of pupils adopted a suitable strategy for the question, though not always obtaining an acceptable answer. There were no differences between the sexes on either answer or method.

2.71   Finally, pupils were asked if they could think of another method of finding the volume of the tin.

9.   "*If you could use anything you like, how would you find the volume of the tin more accurately in terms of the volume of the cube?*"

| Answers | Boys % | Girls % | Total % |
|---|---|---|---|
| * Fill tin with liquid, see how much will fill small box | 17 | 14 | 15 |
| * Calculate volume of tin and cube, divide | 3 | 5 | 4 |
| * Using measuring cylinder and liquid, find volume of tin and small box, divide | 5 | 1 | 3 |
| Use measuring cylinder and liquid, no reference to cube | 16 | 6 | 11 |
| Vague "use liquid" statement | 3 | 3 | 3 |
| Use $\pi r^2 h$, no reference to cube | 14 | 16 | 15 |
| Other incorrect | 26 | 37 | 32 |
| No response | 16 | 18 | 17 |

2.72   The use of a liquid was a popular suggestion but not all pupils remembered that the cube was still being used as the unit of volume. Similarly, most of the pupils who suggested using the formula ($\pi r^2 h$) for a cylinder omitted to state how the answer could be converted to the required units. Pupils who did not refer to the unit cube were prompted:

---

Prompt  "*Remember we are using the cube as a unit of volume*".

---

This prompt was given to 23 per cent of pupils and half of these were then able to describe a correct method.

2.73   Of the large proportion of responses classified as "other incorrect", a number of them were descriptions of incorrect formulae and some pupils simply replied "*Use the formula*". Others suggested measuring the diameter or circumference of the tin without any further explanation.

*Testers' comments*

2.74   Before the survey, several testers were concerned at the use of the word "volume" when the correct term should have been "capacity". This was a deliberate policy since it was thought that the word "capacity" would not be understood by all 15 year olds. During the survey there were no instances recorded of pupils trying to find the amount of metal used to make the tin, as a strict interpretation of the word "volume" in the final questions would require. Apart from this criticism, testers generally considered the topic satisfactory and reported that many pupils found it enjoyable.

*Differences between boys and girls*

2.75   Only question 6 produced a significant difference in success rates between the sexes. Here, 58 per cent of the boys and 46 per cent of the girls were able to state that the true volume of a sphere was less than the fraction obtained by fitting the spheres into the small perspex box. There was no pattern in the differences between boys and girls on the other questions.

2.76    The results of testers' ratings are shown in Figure 2.6.

**Figure 2.6**    *Capacity/volume topic: testers' ratings of pupils.*

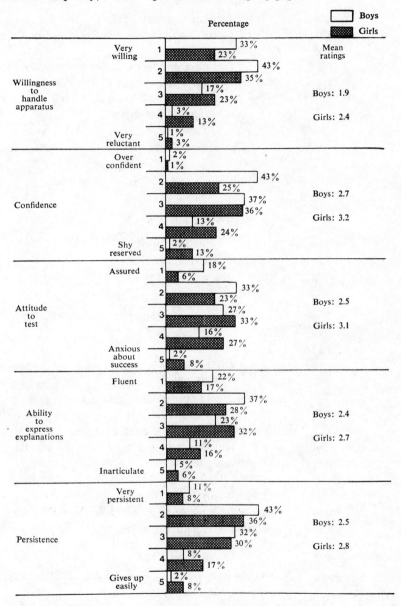

The graphs illustrate the differences in the assessments made for boys and girls. Boys were rated more positively than girls on all scales.

**Symmetry**

2.77    This topic assessed pupils' understanding of reflection through a series of questions involving paper folding and the use of a mirror.

2.78    The first question required the pupil to decide what symmetrical pattern would result from a sequence of folding and cutting a piece of paper.

Pupil and tester have similar sheets of paper ($\frac{1}{3}$ A4).

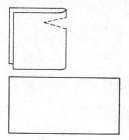

1.  Pupil has pencil (no ruler).
    "*I want you to watch while I fold and cut my piece of paper.*"
    "*This piece of paper was like yours before I folded it and cut a piece out of it. Draw on your piece of paper what this will look like when it's opened out. Draw the fold line as well.*"

| Results | Boys<br>% | Girls<br>% | Total<br>% |
|---|---|---|---|
| * Reasonable attempt | 62 | 46 | 54 |
| Clearly incorrect in 1 or more aspects | 27 | 38 | 33 |
| Draws small version of pattern | 5 | 4 | 4 |
| Other | 4 | 4 | 4 |
| Pupil's work not returned | 2 | 8 | 5 |

2.79   Guidelines were produced which defined what was to be considered as "reasonable". These specified the position of the fold line and the shape, size, symmetry and position of the diamond on the paper. Thus, although the results quoted above are reliable in that the same criteria were used to assess each pupil's attempt, it should be noted that a different set of guidelines would produce different percentages of pupils in each category.

2.80   When pupils had completed their drawing they were asked to unfold the tester's paper to check their attempt. In this way it was hoped that pupils would appreciate any errors or inaccuracies in their drawing before attempting the next question.

Pupil and tester have fresh sheets of paper.

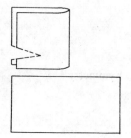

2.  "*Now I'm going to fold and cut another piece of paper like yours. Draw on your piece of paper what this will look like when it's opened out and also draw the fold line.*"

| Results | Boys % | Girls % | Total % |
|---|---|---|---|
| * Reasonable attempt | 72 | 59 | 66 |
| Clearly incorrect in 1 or more aspects | 14 | 16 | 15 |
| Draws small version of pattern | 3 | 4 | 3 |
| Other | 8 | 13 | 11 |
| Pupil's work not returned | 3 | 8 | 5 |

2.81   The guidelines used to assess pupils' performance on this question were identical to those used on the first question and the increase in success rate is probably attributable to the opportunity given to pupils to compare their first drawing with the cut piece of paper.

2.82   The next question required the pupils to fold and cut a piece of paper to produce a given pattern:

3.   Present S1 [◇  ◇] and plain $\frac{1}{3}$ A4 sheet.

*"Fold and cut your piece of paper so that you see this pattern when it's unfolded again."*

Results of question 3 ( *figures in italics are percentages*)

|  | (i) | (ii) | (iii) | (iv) | (v) | (vi) |  |  |
|---|---|---|---|---|---|---|---|---|
| Method \ Answer | 2 parallel folds, correct cut | 2 perpendicular folds, correct cut | Other correct | 2 folds 2 cuts | 1 lengthwise fold, 2 cuts | Attempts to push in scissors | Other inaccurate | Total |
| Reasonable* attempt | 21 | 4 | 5 | 16 | 8 | — | 1 | 55 |
| Clear mistakes but 2 holes | — | — | — | 5 | — | — | 6 | 11 |
| Other | — | — | — | — | — | 16 | 11 | 27 |
| Total | 21 | 4 | 5 | 21 | 8 | 16 | 18 | 93 |
|  |  |  |  |  |  | No response |  | 7 |

**Figure 2.7** *Illustrations of some of the methods used on question 3.*

(i)  2 parallel folds, correct cut.

(ii)  2 perpendicular folds, correct cut.

fold in half

fold in half again, cut.

fold in half

fold in half again (lengthwise), cut.

(iv)  2 folds, 2 cuts

(v)  1 lengthwise fold, 2 cuts.

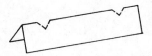

estimate centre, fold each end in, cut along each fold.

2.83  Equal proportions of boys and girls produced attempts classified as "reasonable". The criteria for assessing the pupils' work were similar to those used on the first two questions, specifying allowable margins of error for the shape, size, position and symmetry of the diamonds.

2.84  There were some differences in the methods chosen to attempt this question by boys and girls. Method (i) involving two parallel folds and one cut was adopted by 17 per cent of the boys and 25 per cent of the girls. 27 per cent of the boys and 15 per cent of the girls chose method (iv) which required some estimation as two separate folds and cuts were made.

2.85  Testers were instructed to follow a series of prompts in cases when pupils folded the paper once and then attempted to push the scissors in.

---

Prompt for question 3.
        If pupil attempts to push scissors into paper prompt
        *"Can you think of a way of doing it without pushing your scissors into the paper?"*
        If not prompt
        *"You can fold it more than once if you want."*

---

After these prompts a further 11 per cent produced "reasonable" attempts using one of the satisfactory methods.

2.86 The next set of questions involved the use of a mirror to assess pupils' understanding of symmetry.

---

4. Present S2 ⬚ and mirror. Place mirror successively in 4 positions.
*"What happens when I put the mirror in the different positions?"*

---

2.87 The tester placed the mirror successively along the vertical and horizontal lines of symmetry and along each diagonal. The purpose of the question was to establish that the pupil appreciated that for only two positions of the mirror – along the axes of symmetry – was the reflection in the mirror the same as the pattern on the paper.
Initial responses are listed below:

|  | Boys % | Girls % | Total % |
|---|---|---|---|
| * Pattern same for vertical/horizontal, different for diagonals | 67 | 70 | 69 |
| Other | 33 | 27 | 30 |
| No response | 0 | 3 | 1 |

2.88 Those pupils who failed to appreciate the difference between the two sets of lines were prompted as below:

---

Prompt for question 4.
    If pupil does not indicate difference between mirror on lines of symmetry and non-lines of symmetry, place mirror along a line of symmetry and ask
    *"Does the pattern change?"*
    Repeat with non-line of symmetry.

---

After this, a further 27 per cent of pupils were able to state the difference between the two sets of lines.

2.89 Having established the special properties of the vertical and horizontal lines, the next question was merely to see how many pupils were familiar with the term "symmetry".

---

5. Present S3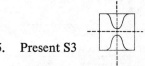

*"When the mirror is placed along these lines, the pattern remains the same."*
Demonstrate again what happens in these 2 positions.
*"What are these lines called?"*

---

| Results | Boys % | Girls % | Total % |
|---|---|---|---|
| * Lines of symmetry | 44 | 42 | 43 |
| * Mirror Lines | 5 | 2 | 3 |
| Vertical, horizontal/ parallel/ axes | 12 | 17 | 15 |
| Other | 15 | 15 | 15 |
| No response | 24 | 24 | 24 |

2.90  For the next question, pupils were required to draw the lines of symmetry on a pattern, though the word "symmetry" was deliberately avoided so as not to deter pupils unfamiliar with the term.

6.  Present S (4) 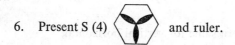 and ruler.

"*Draw the positions of the mirror where the pattern remains the same.*"
Present mirror
"*You can use the mirror if you like.*"

| Results | Boys % | Girls % | Total % |
|---|---|---|---|
| * 3 correct lines, no incorrect | 60 | 51 | 56 |
| 1 or 2 correct lines, no incorrect | 11 | 19 | 15 |
| Other | 20 | 23 | 21 |
| No response | 9 | 7 | 8 |

2.91  Of those who drew the correct lines, about a quarter did not use the mirror, but almost all other pupils chose to experiment with the mirror before drawing any lines.

2.92  Pupils were then asked two questions requiring them to draw a line of symmetry on a pattern without using a mirror.

7.  Remove mirror (leave ruler).

Present S (5) and S (6)

"*Draw, as accurately as you can, a line on here (S5) where you would put a mirror to make this pattern (S6).*"

| Results | Boys % | Girls % | Total % |
|---|---|---|---|
| * Correct line measures width of pattern | 30 | 27 | 28 |
| * Correct line, does not measure | 26 | 24 | 25 |
| Total correct | 56 | 51 | 53 |
| Incorrect line, measures width of pattern | 6 | 2 | 4 |
| Incorrect line, does not measure | 30 | 43 | 37 |
| Other | 7 | 4 | 6 |
| No response | 1 | 0 | 0 |

8. Present another S (5) and S (7)

"*Draw, as accurately as you can, a line on here (S5) where you would put a mirror to make this pattern (S7).*"

| Results | Boys % | Girls % | Total % |
|---|---|---|---|
| * Correct line, measures width of pattern | 42 | 36 | 39 |
| * Correct line, does not measure | 29 | 29 | 29 |
| Total correct | 71 | 65 | 68 |
| Incorrect line, measures width of pattern | 4 | 1 | 2 |
| Incorrect line, does not measure | 18 | 30 | 24 |
| Other | 7 | 4 | 6 |

2.93   Caution needs to be used when interpreting these results, since for each question a region was defined within which answers were considered correct. These regions took into account the distance between the dots on the patterns. It was considered that lines drawn outside the regions were clearly unacceptable. For marking purposes, each region was printed onto an acetate sheet which was then placed over the pupil's drawing. Clearly, different regions could have been devised which would produce different results. Indeed, the difference in success rates between questions 7 and 8 could be entirely due to the different limits which were counted as correct on each drawing. Figure 2.8 shows the regions used.

**Figure 2.8**   *Templates used for marking questions 7 and 8*

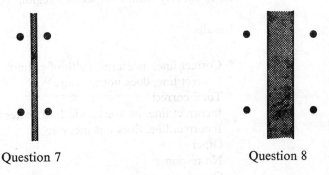

Question 7                                 Question 8

2.94 It is interesting to note that more pupils measured the width of the pattern in question 8 than in question 7 (41 per cent compared with 32 per cent). It could be that, because the dots were further apart in question 8, more pupils thought it necessary to use a ruler, whereas a visual estimate was considered feasible in question 7.

2.95 Almost all pupils whose drawings were classified as incorrect had, nevertheless, drawn a line parallel to the dots, indicating that they appreciated in which direction the mirror should be placed.

2.96 After these two questions, the pupil was presented with a mirror and asked to check both drawings. In this way it was hoped that pupils would be aware of any errors they had made before tackling question 9.

---

9.  Present another S (5) and S (8) and remove mirror.

    *"Draw, as accurately as you can, a line on here (S5) where you would put a mirror to make this pattern (S8)."*

---

2.97 Figure 2.9 below shows the region that was used to define correct responses.

**Figure 2.9**  *Template used for marking question 9.*

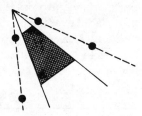

Lines entirely within the shaded region were judged as acceptable.

| Results | Boys | Girls | Total |
|---|---|---|---|
| | % | % | % |
| * Correct line, measures width of pattern | 42 | 35 | 39 |
| * Correct line, does not measure | 40 | 34 | 37 |
| Total correct | 82 | 69 | 76 |
| Incorrect line, measures width of pattern | 1 | 1 | 1 |
| Incorrect line, does not measure | 13 | 23 | 18 |
| Other | 2 | 2 | 2 |
| No response | 1 | 2 | 1 |
| Question not put | 1 | 3 | 2 |

2.98 The opportunity given to pupils to check their drawings for questions 7 and 8 did not influence the methods used to attempt question 9. The proportion of pupils who measured the width of the pattern in question 9 (40 per cent) was almost identical to that in question 8.

2.99 The final question on the topic required pupils to use the properties of a line of symmetry to construct a pattern.

10. Remove mirror.
Present S (9) ＿＿＼＿＿＿ and protractor and compasses.
"*Imagine this dotted line is a mirror line. Draw, as accurately as you can, the reflection of this line.*" (point to it)

Results of question 10 ( *figures in italics are percentages*)

| Method / Answer | Measures* with ruler and protractor | Measures* with compasses and protractor | Measures* perpendicular distance | Measures angle but not length | Measures length but not angle | No measuring | Other | Total |
|---|---|---|---|---|---|---|---|---|
| *⟶ Accurate | 22 | 11 | 15 | — | — | — | 1 | 49 |
| ⟶ Inaccurate | — | — | — | 13 | 1 | 11 | 1 | 26 |
| ＿∨＿ | 1 | 1 | — | 5 | — | 2 | — | 9 |
| ＿╳＿ | — | 1 | — | 3 | 2 | 6 | — | 12 |
| Other | — | — | — | — | — | 3 | — | 3 |
| Total | 23 | 13 | 15 | 21 | 3 | 22 | 2 | 99 |
| | | | | | | No response | | 1 |

2.100   The table of results shows that three-quarters of pupils knew where to draw the reflection of the line, although not always with the required degree of accuracy. Further analysis of these results shows a marked difference between boys and girls.

|  |  | Boys % | Girls % | Total % |
|---|---|---|---|---|
| --〉--- | accurate | 55 | 43 | 49 |
| --〉--- | angle and/or length not the same | 21 | 31 | 26 |
| Total with correct strategy | | 76 | 74 | 75 |

Thus, although almost equal proportions of boys and girls knew where to draw the reflection of the line, boys were more accurate than girls.

2.101   In the 1979 version of the Symmetry topic, the wording used in question 10 was different from that given above. The pattern of results also showed a marked variation from those discussed above:

10.   Present S (9)   __＼___   and protractor and compasses. Remove mirror.

   "Complete this diagram accurately so that the dotted line is a line of symmetry."

| Results (1979 Survey) |  | Boys % | Girls % | Total % |
|---|---|---|---|---|
| --〉-- | accurate | 43 | 34 | 39 |
| --〉-- | angle and/or length not the same | 14 | 8 | 11 |
| __V__ | | 3 | 5 | 4 |
| --✕-- | | 25 | 40 | 32 |
| Other | | 6 | 4 | 5 |
| No response | | 9 | 9 | 9 |

2.102   The above results from the 1979 survey show that only 50 per cent of pupils adopted the correct strategy when the term "symmetry" was used in the question, compared with 75 per cent when asked for a reflection to be drawn. Another striking feature of the results is the proportion of pupils who chose to extend the line through the dotted line. 32 per cent did this when the question asked for the diagram to be completed so that the dotted line was a line of symmetry, whereas only 12 per cent made the same mistake when the question described the dotted line as a mirror line and asked for the reflection to be drawn.

*Testers' comments*

2.103   Some testers raised doubts about the wording used for question 10 in the 1980 survey. Since the dotted line was described as a mirror line, they felt that pupils would interpret the line as a beam of light and draw its reflection thus:

The results suggest that some pupils did consider the question in this way since the proportion making this error was 9 per cent, compared with 4 per cent when the line was described as a line of symmetry.

2.104   On the whole, testers thought that the topic provided a thorough assessment of line symmetry. The material was generally considered to be suitable even for those pupils who had not studied symmetry as part of their mathematics curriculum. Some testers remarked that the accuracy required in answers was not stressed adequately in the questions and that, if this point had been emphasised more strongly, more pupils might have chosen to use the ruler to measure the width of the pattern in, for example, questions 7, 8 and 9.

*Differences between boys and girls*

2.105   Boys' success rates were significantly higher than girls' on the first two questions in which pupils were asked to draw the patterns that would result from a sequence of folding and cutting pieces of paper. There was also a significant difference between the sexes in question 9 which required a line of symmetry to be drawn on a pattern without the use of a mirror. Here, 82 per cent of boys and 69 per cent of girls were successful. No other significant differences were recorded, although boys' success rates were higher than girls' on all other questions except number 4, which asked pupils to explain the different effect of placing a mirror along a line of symmetry of a pattern compared with a non-line of symmetry.

2.106   Testers' ratings of pupils' approaches to the topic also showed differences between boys and girls. (see Figure 2.10)

2.107   The most notable differences were in the scales assessing confidence and attitude to the topic, where boys were rated as more confident and assured than girls. The results also showed that boys were rated as more willing to handle the apparatus than girls, which might account for some of the differences in success rates.

[1]Fennema, E(Ed)
*Mathematics learning:
what research says about
sex differences.*
Mathematics Education
Reports, Ohio State
University, 1975.

2.108   Questions 1 and 2 involved visualising a change in the presented materials by mental manipulation. Research studies have often shown that boys perform better than girls on such tasks.[1]

**Figure 2.10**   *Symmetry topic: testers' ratings of pupils.*

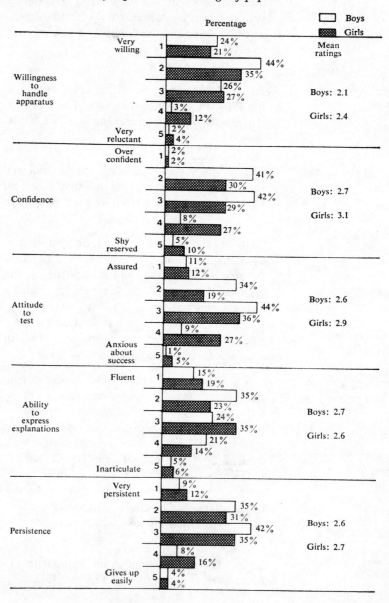

## Scores on practical topics and written concepts and skills tests

**Relationships between
1980 practical topics**

2.109   For each pupil in the sample, a score was obtained for each of the practical topics attempted. The scores were obtained by awarding one mark for each acceptable answer or method and then totalling a pupil's marks for the topic. Each pupil took two or three practical topics and in order to gain some idea of the consistency of the level of pupils' performance, topic scores were correlated. The design of the practical survey (paragraphs 2.3 – 2.11) meant that the problem solving topics could only be correlated with two others, while the remaining topics could be correlated with four or five others. The results are shown in Table 2.3.

**Table 2.3** *Correlations between practical topics*

| | Angles | Area | Calculators | Capacity/Volume | Dominoes | Journey to France | Length | Mass | Probability | Symmetry | Tiles |
|---|---|---|---|---|---|---|---|---|---|---|---|
| Angles | | — | — | — | — | — | 0.65 | 0.60 | 0.49 | — | 0.44 |
| Area | — | | 0.64 | 0.51 | — | — | — | — | — | 0.61 | 0.58 |
| Calculators | — | 59 | | 0.59 | — | — | 0.67 | — | 0.49 | 0.74 | — |
| Capacity/Volume | — | 56 | 109 | | 0.63 | — | 0.58 | — | — | 0.42 | — |
| Dominoes | — | — | — | 111 | | — | — | — | 0.37 | — | — |
| Journey to France | — | — | — | — | — | | — | 0.45 | — | — | — |
| Length | 51 | — | 222 | 111 | — | — | | 0.41 | 0.53 | 0.59 | — |
| Mass | 108 | — | — | — | — | 117 | 51 | | 0.49 | — | — |
| Probability | 55 | — | 112 | — | 112 | — | 114 | 56 | | — | — |
| Symmetry | — | 117 | 59 | 56 | — | 109 | — | — | — | | — |
| Tiles | 114 | 106 | — | — | — | — | — | — | — | — | |

Correlation coefficients are given in the upper triangular half of the table. The numbers of pupils used to compute each coefficient are given in the lower half of the table.

2.110   One further consequence of the design of the survey was that eight of the correlations were based on the scores of 50–60 pupils, twelve were based on the scores of 105–120 pupils and one was based on the scores of 222 pupils. All but one of the correlations obtained were statistically significant at the 0.1 per cent level. The correlations range from 0.37 to 0.74, with the Probability topic tending to have the lowest correlations with other topics and the Calculators topic tending to have the highest.

**Relationships between scores on written concepts and skills tests and practical topics**

2.111   The pupils who took a practical test were a sub-sample of those who took the written concepts and skills tests and so it is possible to compare performance on the two modes of testing. Since there were 25 written tests, each consisting of a selection of items from three different sub-categories (see Table 3.1, page 53), a procedure was needed to take account of the varying difficulty of these tests. A scaling technique was used to transform pupils' scores onto a common scale and the scores thus obtained were correlated with the practical topic scores (see paragraph 3.6 for details of the scaling technique). The results are given below in Table 2.4.

**Table 2.4**   *Correlations between practical topic scores and scaled scores on written concepts and skills tests*

| Topic | Correlation | Number of pupils |
|---|---|---|
| Angles | 0.73 | 220 |
| Area | 0.55 | 221 |
| Calculators | 0.80 | 279 |
| Capacity/volume | 0.61 | 272 |
| Dominoes | 0.54 | 219 |
| Journey to France | 0.57 | 224 |
| Length | 0.65 | 276 |
| Mass | 0.47 | 223 |
| Probability | 0.50 | 279 |
| Symmetry | 0.68 | 224 |
| Tiles | 0.41 | 224 |

2.112   The highest correlations obtained involve topics with a high skills content: Calculators, Angles and Symmetry, while the lowest correlations involve topics with a high problem solving strategy content: Tiles, Mass and Dominoes.

2.113   For the three topics discussed in this chapter, a more detailed analysis of performance on the two modes of testing was made. Scatterplots were produced showing pupils' scores on the practical topic, expressed as a percentage, against their scaled score on the written tests. Figure 2.11 below shows the scores for those pupils who took the Area topic.

**Figure 2.11** *Scatterplot of Area topic scores and scaled written test scores*

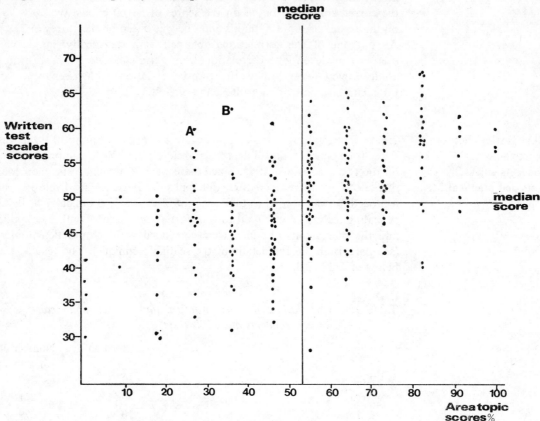

*A, B: Pupils whose scores are discussed in the text.*

2.114    The scripts of certain pupils who had inconsistent results for the written tests and the Area topic were studied in detail to see if the mistakes made would indicate any general problems pupils had with the concept of area. The scripts chosen were those of pupils whose written test scores were high but whose performance on the Area topic was below average. Two such scripts are discussed below.

2.115    Pupil A:               Boy
       Area topic score            27% (8th percentile)
       Written test scaled score   59   (87th percentile)

The pupil gave the correct answers for the areas of the first two shapes – triangle B and the parallelogram D. However, both answers were obtained by making a visual estimate and no attempt was made to check the areas by placing the unit triangle over the shapes. When asked which of shapes A – D were equal in area to the square E, he initially gave only one correct answer but, after prompting, gave the full response. The next question asked for the area of the rectangle using a tile as a unit of area. He gave an incorrect response of 6 units, due to rather haphazard placement of the tile on the rectangle. Finally, he gave an acceptable estimate for the area of the irregular shape but was unable to suggest a method for getting a more accurate answer. When presented with the same shape drawn on a grid, he could not use it to find the area.

2.116   The tester rated pupil A at the mid-point of each of the five-point scales assessing approach to the topic.

2.117   Pupil B:                              Girl
         Area topic score                    36% (16th percentile)
         Written test scaled score           63    (95th percentile)

This pupil's responses followed a similar pattern to those discussed above. The areas of shapes B and D were given without handling the shapes. Only shape C was identified from A – D as being equal in area to the square E. The area of the rectangle was estimated incorrectly as 4 units, without using the unit tile. She gave an acceptable estimate of the area of the irregular shape but could not suggest a method for obtaining a more accurate answer. Although she adopted a suitable strategy when presented with the shape drawn on a grid, her answer was below the range considered as acceptable. This pupil was rated by the tester as rather shy and anxious about her success, but at the mid-point on the other scales.

2.118   Figure 2.12 below shows the Capacity/volume topic scores plotted against the written test scaled scores.

**Figure 2.12** *Scatterplot of Capacity/volume topic scores and scaled written test scores*

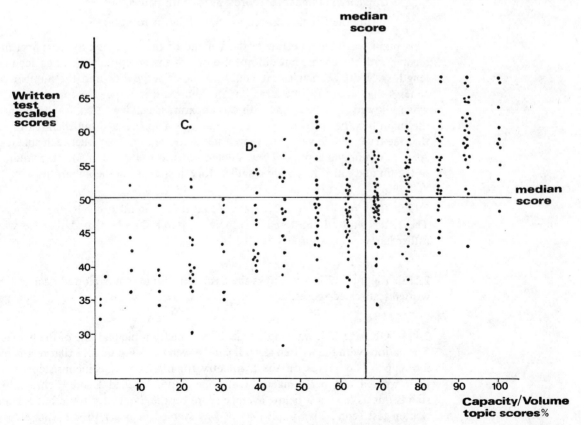

*C, D: Pupils whose scores are discussed in the text.*

2.119   Again, the scripts of those pupils with inconsistent results were examined in detail and two of them are described below.

2.120   Pupil C:                              Girl
    Capacity/volume topic score   23% (5th percentile)
    Written test scaled score        61   (90th percentile)

This pupil gave acceptable responses to the questions concerning the volume of the large perspex box but was unable to cope with the rest of the topic. She could not describe how to use the small box to find out how many spheres would fill the large box. Although she fitted 8 spheres into the small box, her method for using that result to work out how many would fit into the large box was obscure. She took the dimensions of the large box, $5 \times 4 \times 3$, and then incorrectly worked out $(5 \times 8) \times (4 \times 8) \times 3$ to give 3780. When asked for the volume of a sphere, she replied "$\frac{1}{3}\pi r^2$", rather than using the fact that 8 spheres made one unit of volume. She continued to think in terms of formulae when asked to find the volume of the cylindrical tin and could not use the apparatus provided.

2.121   Pupil D:                              **Boy**
    Capacity/volume topic score   39% (14th percentile)
    Written test scaled score        57   (80th percentile)

This pupil was able to estimate the volume of the large box and confirm his answer with the cubes, but did not use one of the acceptable methods such as length $\times$ width $\times$ height. He could not describe how to find the number of spheres that would fill the large box but did manage to get the correct answer when allowed to experiment with the apparatus. Having fitted 7 spheres into the small box, he correctly gave the volume of a sphere as $\frac{1}{7}$ but then reasoned that the true volume would be more than that due to the gaps between spheres. As with the previous pupil, he was determined to use a formula for the volume of the tin and failed to obtain a satisfactory answer using the apparatus.

2.122   Both pupils C and D were rated positively on all scales by their testers. The tester who administered the topic to pupil D commented that he was rather hasty in his approach to questions.

2.123   Figure 2.13 below shows the Symmetry topic scores plotted against the written test scaled scores.

2.124   On page 45 it was noted that the Symmetry topic had one of the highest correlations with the written tests. It can be seen from Figure 2.13 that relatively few pupils had scores on the Symmetry topic which were inconsistent with their written test performance. Only one pupil, labelled E on Figure 2.13, stands out as having a below average score on the Symmetry topic but a high written test score. This pupil's script was studied in order to see what errors had been made.

**Figure 2.13** *Scatterplot of Symmetry topic scores and scaled written test scores*

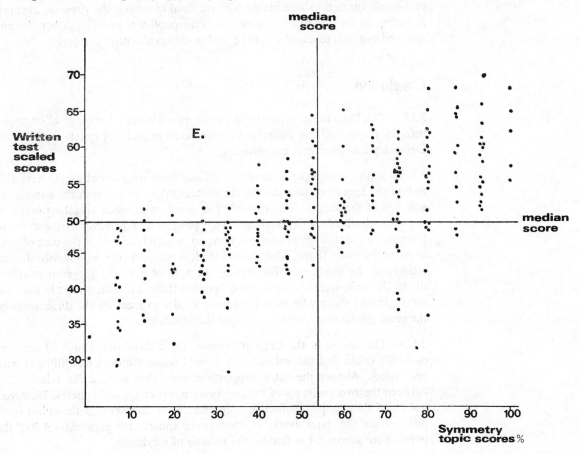

*E: Pupil whose score is discussed in the text.*

2.125   Pupil E:                           Girl
    Symmetry topic score        *27%* (16th percentile)
    Written test scaled score    61   (88th percentile)

The initial questions on folding and cutting a piece of paper had not been answered successfully. She did not appreciate the difference between placing

a mirror along a line of symmetry of the pattern [figure] as compared with

the diagonals. After prompting, she recognised the difference but could only describe the line of symmetry as *"intersecting lines"* when asked if they had a

special name. She joined opposite vertices when presented with [figure]

and asked to draw the positions of the mirror where the pattern remains the same. The series of questions concerning the position of the mirror line that would produce a given pattern of dots were all tackled without using the ruler to measure the width of the pattern. The lines drawn were all outside the regions designated as acceptable. On the final question, she drew an accurate reflection of the line in the mirror line. This pupil was rated as rather shy and reserved but was assessed as at the mid-point on all other categories.

## Conclusion

2.126   The three topics reported in this chapter illustrate the range of strategies used by pupils and the difficulties encountered in tackling questions from the Geometry and Measures categories.

2.127   In the Area topic, between a half and three-quarters of pupils were able to find the area of certain shapes, the success rates varying with the complexity and size of the shape. The proportion of pupils who made visual estimates of the areas declined as larger shapes were presented. When comparing areas of triangles, a parallelogram and a square, some pupils arranged the unit of area to cover the given shape, while others made a comparison which involved some estimation. Methods used for finding the area of a rectangle, given a square tile as the unit, were evenly divided between those who fitted the tile over the rectangle and those who used the tile as a ruler to measure the dimensions of the rectangle so that they could apply the algorithm.

2.128   The results of the Capacity/volume topic show that about 70 per cent of pupils could find the volume of a cuboid without completely filling it with unit cubes. Almost the same proportion were able to give the relationship between the two measures of volume being used: cubes and spheres. However, not all of these pupils realised the significance of the fact that the cubes completely filled the space available whereas the spheres left gaps. About half the pupils were successful in finding the volume of a cylinder.

2.129   Pupils' understanding of the construction of patterns by folding and cutting paper was assessed in the Symmetry topic. Between 55 per cent and 65 per cent of pupils were successful within given margins of error. A series of questions requiring pupils to draw the lines of symmetry on patterns produced success rates varying from around 50 per cent to 75 per cent. The availability of a mirror for checking did not affect performance levels. There was some evidence that the complexity of the pattern influenced pupils' decisions on whether to use a ruler to measure the width of the pattern. Pupils' usage of the properties of a line of symmetry to construct a pattern was found to depend very much on the wording of the question.

2.130   Testers' ratings of pupils' approaches to the topics showed considerable differences in the assessments made for boys and girls. On the scales assessing confidence, attitude to the test and willingness to handle apparatus, boys' ratings were consistently higher than girls'. There were also differences between the sexes on the scales assessing persistence and ability to express explanations, though these differences were smaller than those noted on the other scales.

2.131   Pupils generally responded well to the unfamiliar assessment methods and many testers commented on the pupils' cooperation and enthusiasm.

It was felt by some testers that the practical tests were not looked upon as mathematics by some pupils, because they did not reflect their normal classroom experiences. Examples of such remarks are:

> *"I was never interested before but I like this"*
> *"This is good. I can talk about maths but I can never write it down."*
> *"The tests were enjoyable – not a bit like lessons."*

2.132   Many testers spoke of the survey as a rewarding and valuable experience. Testers welcomed the opportunity to work with pupils from different schools and remarked that through individual interviews they had gained a useful insight into pupils' thinking and the problems encountered. One particular point noted was the difficulties pupils had with mathematical terms. For example, in the Capacity/volume topic some pupils referred to the spheres as *"circles"* while others spoke of finding the area rather than the volume of the objects. When testers probed to discover the methods used in certain questions a typical response was *"I'll show you"* rather than giving a verbal description to justify their answer.

[1]*Mathematics counts,* HMSO, (1982).

2.133   The Cockcroft Committee in their report[1] stated that oral work and discussion should be an essential part of all mathematics teaching. They stressed the value of practical activity and investigational work for pupils of all ages and abilities. In their comments on the secondary curriculum, the Committee emphasised the need to read, write and talk about mathematics in a wide variety of ways and proposed that pupils should be encouraged to discuss and justify the methods which they use. This chapter has provided some illustrations of the value of this approach with 15 year olds.

2.134   Some testers commented on the benefits they considered the practical tests offered:

> *"As a vehicle for learning, games and practical situations that can arise in mathematics offer a great deal for many children".*
>
> *"I am convinced that pupils must have more practical experience, despite the pressure of examination syllabus contents – they could be so much more aware and probably more inventive."*

2.135   One-to-one interviews can provide detailed information about pupils' performance which adds to the general picture obtained from the more conventional written tests.

# 3 The written tests: sub-category scores and background variables

## The 1980 survey tests

3.1   The design for the 1980 secondary survey tests was similar to that used in the 1978 and 1979 surveys. As before, a total of 25 different tests was used but, in 1980, items from only 13, rather than 15, sub-categories were included. This was in order to allow extended coverage in three of the sub-categories to give a more detailed picture of performance in those areas. The three sub-categories chosen for the increased coverage in 1980 were Number concepts, Unit measures and Descriptive geometry. Table 3.1 shows the sub-categories appearing in each of the 25 tests and also the number of tests each sub-category appeared in. Each test contained around 50 items, with each item appearing in two tests, so that every sub-category part was made up of around 17 items. The space for the extra items was created by not including the sub-category Rate and ratio and by combining Probability and Statistics into one sub-category. Some items from Rate and ratio, were, however, included in the 1980 survey in the Number applications sub-category so that this sub-category is larger than it was in the two previous surveys. It is intended to continue this policy of giving more detailed coverage to different areas of the curriculum in subsequent surveys so that by the end of the series of five surveys it will be possible to give a detailed picture of performance in major areas of the curriculum.

[1]See Chapter 3 of *Mathematics development. Secondary survey report No. 1.* 1980.

3.2   The number of items used in each sub-category is shown in Table 3.2. A more detailed description of the design of the tests and the model for this design can be found in the first secondary survey report[1].

3.3   In this chapter, performance on the written tests in the 1980 survey is considered against the background variables, while in Chapter 4 performance on some clusters of items of related content is described.

**Table 3.1** *Summary of test design showing sub-categories used in each test.*

| Group | TEST NO. | | 1 | 2 | 3 | 4 | 5 | 6 | 7 | 8 | 9 | 10 | 11 | 12 | 13 | 14 | 15 | 16 | 17 | 18 | 19 | 20 | 21 | 22 | 23 | 24 | 25 |
|---|---|---|---|---|---|---|---|---|---|---|---|---|---|---|---|---|---|---|---|---|---|---|---|---|---|---|---|
| NUMBER | Number concepts | F | F1 | F2 | F3 | F4 | F5 | | | | | | | | | | | | | F6 | | | | | F7 | F8 | | |
| | Number skills | H | H1 | | | | | H2 | H3 | H4 | H5 | | | | | | | | | | | | | | | | | |
| | Number applications | J | J1 | | | | | J2 | | | | J3 | J4 | J5 | | | J6 | | | | | | | | | | | J7 |
| MEASURES | Unit measures | R | | | R1 | | | | | | | | | | R2 | R3 | R4 | R5 | | | R6 | | | | R7 | R8 | | |
| | Mensuration | Q | | | | Q1 | | | | Q2 | Q3 | | | | Q4 | | | | Q5 | | | | | | | | | |
| | General algebra | M | | | | | M1 | | | | M2 | M3 | | | | M4 | | | M5 | | | | | | | | | |
| | Traditional algebra | U | | U1 | | | | | | | | | | U2 | | | U3 | | | U4 | U5 | | | | | | | |
| ALGEBRA | Modern algebra | N | | N1 | | | | | | | N2 | | | | | | | N3 | | | N4 | N5 | | | | | | |
| | Graphical algebra | V | | | V1 | | | | | V2 | | | V3 | | | | | | | | | V4 | V5 | | | | | |
| | Descriptive geometry | P | | | | P1 | | | P2 | | | | | P3 | | P4 | | | | | | P5 | P6 | | P7 | P8 | | |
| GEOMETRY | Modern geometry | B | | | | B1 | B2 | | | | | | | | B3 | | | | | B4 | B5 | | | | | | | |
| | Trigonometry | S | | | | | | | | | | S1 | | | | | | | | | | | | S2 | S3 | S4 | | |
| STATISTICS | Statistics probability | W | | | | | | | W1 | | | | | | | | | W2 | | | | W3 | W4 | | | | | W5 |

**Table 3.2**   *Number of items used within each sub-category for the 1980 survey.*

| Main content category | Sub-category | Number of items |
|---|---|---|
| Number | Concepts | 80 |
| | Skills | 43 |
| | Applications | 63 |
| Measures | Unit | 77 |
| | Mensuration | 41 |
| Algebra | General algebra | 42 |
| | Traditional algebra | 43 |
| | Modern algebra | 41 |
| | Graphical algebra | 42 |
| Geometry | Descriptive geometry | 66 |
| | Modern geometry | 42 |
| | Trigonometry | 31 |
| Probability and statistics | Probability and statistics | 42 |

## Written tests: the sub-category scores

3.4   All the variables used to analyse the 1978 and 1979 results have been used again for 1980 but, in addition, performance is reported against a new variable, that of school catchment area. The results obtained for 1980 are broadly similar to those obtained in 1978 and 1979.

3.5   As described in paragraph 3.1, the collection of items used for the survey was organised into thirteen sub-categories, with each test containing items from three of these. In this chapter, performance on each sub-category is reported against the background variables. To do this, a sub-category score had to be obtained for each grouping of the background variables. This was achieved by converting each pupil's performance on the respective sub-category into a score on a common scale and then averaging these scores across all the pupils who took that sub-category; mean scores for the various sub-divisions of the sample were obtained by averaging across all the pupils within the appropriate sub-division. Thus, pupils taking a test containing items from three sub-categories obtained a separate score for each sub-category and so contributed to the mean scores of these three sub-categories.

3.6   When the tests were constructed, the sub-categories were divided into between four and eight parts and, for each sub-category, the different parts were made as nearly equal in overall difficulty as was possible, but inevitably there is some variation in their respective difficulties. If the proportion correct on each sub-category part were used as a pupil's sub-category score, equal proportions on different parts would not necessarily be equivalent. The particular technique of scaling applied enabled allowances to be made for any variation in the difficulties of the sub-category parts[1]. It should be noted that

[1]The particular scaling technique used here is based on the Rasch model. A brief outline can be found in Appendix 3 of *Mathematical development: primary survey report No. 2.* (HMSO, 1981.)

this scaling is considered within each sub-category so that there is, in effect, a different scale for each sub-category.

3.7 The estimates of performance derived for each pupil using the scaling approach take into account the relative difficulties of the items forming the sub-category. The result of this is that a pupil taking difficult items would be assigned a higher performance measure for a given score than a pupil with an identical raw score but over a set of easy items. Consequently, the average performance measure on all sub-categories will be about the same. However, the measures as reported have been adjusted by the average difficulty of the sub-category. Thus, the mean score of the total sample on each sub-category is a reflection of the particular items which form that sub-category. Hence, the Unit measures sub-category has the highest mean score as it contains more items with a higher success rate than the others, while conversely, the low mean score on Trigonometry is a consequence of it containing items which pupils generally found more difficult. The differences which can be seen in Table 3.4 in the sub-category overall mean scores should be viewed as being dependent on the collection of items it was thought would appropriately reflect the curriculum in each sub-category.

3.8 Items used in the 1980 survey which were included in previous surveys have not been statistically linked to those surveys. Thus, the mean sub-category measures reported here cannot necessarily be considered as being on the same scale as used for previous surveys.

3.9 Figure 3.1 shows the relationship between the scaled scores reported in this chapter and the more familiar way of expressing test scores as a percentage of correct responses. The figure provides an approximate empirical conversion of the scaled scores into their equivalents in terms of the percentage of items in the sub-category which would be answered correctly if all the items in that sub-category were used as a single test. Thus, a mean scaled score of 50 implies that 50 per cent of the items would be answered correctly by the average pupil; a mean scaled score of 45 implies just over 30 per cent of the items would be answered correctly by such a pupil, and so on. In addition, it can be seen from Figure 3.1 that the majority of scaled scores are likely to lie in the range from 35 to 65 scaled units, since this band covers the range of 5 per cent to 95 per cent of items answered correctly.

[1]The scores given in this chapter for each grouping of the background variables (see Table 3.4) are weighted to reflect the estimated population figures. The latter are given in brackets after the sample percentages.

3.10 As part of the information collected from schools, teachers were asked to estimate the likely achievement of each pupil in the sample in public examinations using the following five point scale:

| Group | Percentage of pupils in total sample (estimate of population in brackets)[1] | |
|---|---|---|
| 1 Top grade O-level maths | 14 | (13) |
| 2 Lower grade O-level maths pass or CSE maths equivalent | 25 | (23) |
| 3 Middle grade CSE maths | 21 | (23) |
| 4 Lower grade CSE maths | 22 | (26) |
| 5 Unlikely to be entered for either CSE maths or O-level maths | 15 | (15) |
| Not given | 3 | (–) |

**Figure 3.1**  *Showing the relationship between the scaled scores and the percentage of items which would be answered correctly if all the items in the sub-category were used as a single test.*

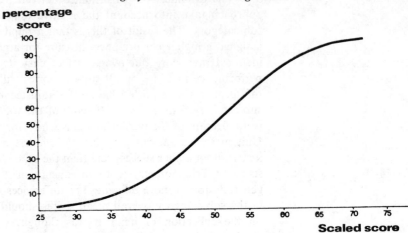

3.11   Table 3.3 shows the mean scores obtained by each achievement group and the overall mean for each sub-category. Mean scores declined consistently through the achievement groups; the differences between the mean scores of each group were significant in every sub-category.

**Table 3.3**  *Mean scaled scores for each sub-category by achievement groups.*

|  |  | Achievement group | | | | | Overall |
|---|---|---|---|---|---|---|---|
|  |  | 1 | 2 | 3 | 4 | 5 | Mean |
| Number | Concepts | 61.9 | 57.7 | 52.4 | 47.6 | 42.6 | 52.0 |
|  | Skills | 60.3 | 55.6 | 50.1 | 45.1 | 41.5 | 50.1 |
|  | Applications | 57.3 | 52.4 | 47.1 | 42.8 | 38.5 | 46.9 |
| Measures | Unit | 60.2 | 57.0 | 52.6 | 48.7 | 44.5 | 52.4 |
|  | Mensuration | 55.0 | 48.5 | 43.7 | 39.9 | 36.4 | 44.1 |
| Algebra | General | 60.5 | 54.8 | 47.9 | 44.1 | 39.7 | 48.8 |
|  | Traditional | 60.5 | 54.2 | 48.2 | 42.9 | 38.4 | 48.3 |
|  | Modern | 57.2 | 53.4 | 47.7 | 44.0 | 40.4 | 48.2 |
|  | Graphical | 55.8 | 49.8 | 44.8 | 41.0 | 36.5 | 44.7 |
| Geometry | Descriptive | 59.7 | 55.0 | 50.6 | 45.7 | 41.2 | 50.0 |
|  | Modern | 54.0 | 49.7 | 44.7 | 40.7 | 37.9 | 44.9 |
|  | Trigonometry | 52.4 | 46.3 | 40.9 | 38.7 | 37.4 | 42.8 |
| Probability and statistics | Probability and statistics | 59.3 | 55.9 | 52.5 | 47.4 | 43.1 | 51.5 |

3.12   As well as showing a high level of agreement between the teachers' estimates of achievement and pupils' performance, Table 3.3. can be used as an illustration of the scale used to report scores in this chapter. By considering the range of mean scores obtained by the five achievement groups and the differences between various groupings of the background variables reported later in this chapter, the table also illustrates the point that the differences between individual pupils are greater than the differences in mean scores between the groupings of the background variables.

## The background variables

3.13   In this section, performance is reported in relation to six characteristics of the schools in the sample. These are:

(i)   Region of the country.

(ii)   Location in a metropolitan or non-metropolitan county.

(iii)   Size of 15-plus age group.

(iv)   Catchment area.

(v)   Pupil/teacher ratio.

(vi)   Percentage of pupils taking free school meals.

Table 3.4 shows the scaled scores obtained by the pupils in each grouping of the background variables for each sub-category, as well as the scores of the whole sample.

3.14   The difference between the mean scaled scores obtained by the pupils in each grouping of the background variables and the mean scaled score obtained for all the pupils who took the sub-category in 1980 are shown in graphical form in Figures 3.2 to 3.10. In each case, an indication is given of the 95 per cent confidence limits: that is, the range within which these differences are most likely to lie for the total population. For example, in Figure 3.2 the mean difference score on Number concepts for the sample in the Midlands is 0.1 (from Table 3.4: 52.1–52.0) while this difference is most likely to lie in the range —1.0 to +1.2.

3.15   It is useful, as a rule of thumb, to note those occasions when there is only a small overlap, or none at all, between two sets of confidence limits. In these cases, the discrepancy between the two mean scores concerned is so large that it is unlikely to have arisen solely from sampling fluctuations and is, thus, likely to be significant in the statistical sense (see Appendix 2).

3.16   It is important to interpret the discrepancies in mean score between the groupings of the background variables in the light of the much larger differences occurring between pupils within the groupings. For example, despite the associations between performance and the area in which a school is situated, there are still many pupils attending schools in city centres whose performance would be high amongst any group of 15 year olds.

**Table 3.4** *Mean scaled scores for each sub-category and background variable.*

| | | | Region | | | | Location | | Size of 15 plus age group* | | | |
|---|---|---|---|---|---|---|---|---|---|---|---|---|
| | | All | North | Mid. | South | Wales | N.I. | Non-Met. | Met. | 4–145 | 146–205 | 206–265 | 266+ |
| **NUMBER** | Concepts | 52.0 | 51.5 | 52.1 | 52.6 | 51.1 | 51.9 | 52.5 | 51.1 | 52.6 | 51.7 | 51.4 | 52.6 |
| | Skills | 50.1 | 48.8 | 50.7 | 50.6 | 49.1 | 52.2 | 50.5 | 49.3 | 50.6 | 49.0 | 49.4 | 50.6 |
| | Applications | 46.9 | 46.4 | 46.3 | 47.9 | 45.6 | 47.0 | 47.4 | 46.0 | 46.6 | 46.6 | 45.9 | 46.6 |
| **MEAS-URES** | Unit | 52.4 | 52.0 | 52.3 | 52.9 | 51.2 | 51.8 | 52.7 | 51.7 | 52.6 | 52.2 | 52.2 | 52.6 |
| | Mensuration | 44.1 | 43.3 | 44.4 | 44.8 | 42.5 | 43.9 | 44.7 | 43.1 | 44.5 | 43.4 | 43.6 | 44.5 |
| **ALGEBRA** | General | 48.8 | 48.2 | 48.8 | 49.4 | 47.6 | 49.3 | 49.3 | 47.8 | 48.8 | 47.7 | 49.2 | 48.8 |
| | Traditional | 48.3 | 47.8 | 48.2 | 49.0 | 46.6 | 48.3 | 48.8 | 47.3 | 48.5 | 47.6 | 47.9 | 48.5 |
| | Modern | 48.2 | 47.2 | 48.3 | 49.0 | 46.2 | 49.2 | 48.8 | 47.1 | 48.0 | 47.6 | 48.0 | 48.0 |
| | Graphical | 44.7 | 44.0 | 44.7 | 45.6 | 42.2 | 44.9 | 45.2 | 43.9 | 44.3 | 44.4 | 44.7 | 44.3 |
| **GEOMETRY** | Descriptive | 50.0 | 49.2 | 49.6 | 51.0 | 48.7 | 49.1 | 50.5 | 49.1 | 50.4 | 49.5 | 49.3 | 50.4 |
| | Modern | 44.9 | 44.1 | 44.4 | 46.1 | 42.4 | 43.8 | 45.4 | 44.0 | 44.6 | 44.1 | 44.8 | 44.6 |
| | Trigonometry | 42.8 | 42.7 | 42.5 | 43.3 | 41.5 | 41.8 | 43.0 | 42.5 | 42.9 | 41.9 | 42.6 | 42.9 |
| **STAT.** | Statistics and probability | 51.5 | 51.0 | 52.0 | 52.0 | 49.5 | 50.4 | 51.8 | 51.0 | 51.7 | 51.1 | 51.3 | 51.7 |

*Maintained sample in England only.
**Maintained sample of England and Wales only
***Maintained sample only.

3.17 Another proviso concerning the data on the background variables must also be mentioned; the variables are not all independent and although comment is made concerning some of the major interactions between them, no detailed analysis of the effects of these interactions is reported here. Work is continuing on the use of more explanatory analyses and, until these are completed, the relationships between the background variables and performance reported here must be interpreted with care. Finally, as with all such studies, a causal relationship cannot be assumed simply because a strong association is reported between any particular background variable and performance. For example, other researchers have reported a substantial correlation between the attitudes of parents to school and the school performance of their children. However, this does not imply that positive parental attitudes are a direct cause of their children's good performance. Indeed, it might equally well be that having successful children promotes positive parental attitudes towards school or that both the parents' attitudes and child's performance depend upon some common factor underlying both variables.

| | Catchment area | | | | Pupil/teacher** ratio | | | Per cent taking free*** school meals | | | Sex of pupil | |
|---|---|---|---|---|---|---|---|---|---|---|---|---|
| Rural | City centre | Est. manuf | Prosp sub. | Less prosp sub. | <15 | 15–17.4 | ≥17.5 | <6 | 6–13.9 | ≥14 | Boys | Girls |
| 52.8 | 49.1 | 52.3 | 55.3 | 50.1 | 50.0 | 51.8 | 52.1 | 53.5 | 50.6 | 48.0 | 52.8 | 51.3 |
| 50.3 | 47.1 | 50.9 | 53.3 | 48.6 | 48.5 | 49.9 | 49.5 | 51.3 | 48.7 | 46.5 | 50.3 | 49.8 |
| 47.8 | 44.4 | 47.0 | 49.8 | 45.4 | 45.5 | 46.8 | 46.3 | 47.9 | 45.7 | 43.9 | 47.7 | 46.2 |
| 53.2 | 49.5 | 52.8 | 55.0 | 50.9 | 50.5 | 52.6 | 51.5 | 53.5 | 50.8 | 49.9 | 53.4 | 51.3 |
| 44.9 | 40.9 | 44.3 | 46.9 | 42.8 | 41.7 | 44.1 | 43.6 | 45.1 | 42.6 | 41.0 | 45.1 | 43.1 |
| 49.1 | 45.7 | 49.4 | 52.5 | 46.9 | 47.5 | 48.7 | 47.7 | 49.8 | 47.1 | 45.9 | 49.2 | 48.4 |
| 49.1 | 45.3 | 48.8 | 52.3 | 49.9 | 46.2 | 48.1 | 47.6 | 49.7 | 46.5 | 44.7 | 48.7 | 47.9 |
| 49.5 | 45.8 | 47.9 | 51.2 | 45.6 | 46.1 | 48.2 | 47.6 | 49.5 | 46.4 | 45.1 | 48.3 | 48.0 |
| 45.6 | 41.2 | 45.6 | 47.8 | 42.9 | 42.5 | 44.8 | 43.9 | 46.1 | 43.4 | 40.8 | 44.9 | 44.5 |
| 50.7 | 45.9 | 51.0 | 53.4 | 48.4 | 49.1 | 49.9 | 49.2 | 51.6 | 48.1 | 46.5 | 51.1 | 48.8 |
| 46.0 | 42.7 | 44.0 | 47.8 | 43.0 | 43.9 | 44.4 | 44.9 | 46.2 | 42.8 | 42.2 | 45.2 | 44.6 |
| 42.6 | 40.6 | 43.8 | 46.0 | 40.8 | 40.9 | 42.8 | 42.2 | 43.9 | 41.3 | 40.1 | 43.1 | 42.5 |
| 52.1 | 49.2 | 51.4 | 54.5 | 49.7 | 49.7 | 51.7 | 51.0 | 52.7 | 50.4 | 48.3 | 52.0 | 51.0 |

**Region**

3.18   The sample was divided into five regions as follows:—

| Group | | Percentage of pupils in the total sample (estimate of population in brackets) | |
|---|---|---|---|
| 1. | North | *21* | *(29)* |
| 2. | Midlands | *16* | *(22)* |
| 3. | South | *31* | *(40)* |
| 4. | Wales | *17* | *(5)* |
| 5. | Northern Ireland | *15* | *(4)* |

3.19   As described in Appendix 1, higher proportions of pupils were sampled in Wales and Northern Ireland compared with England. Thus, the proportions of pupils in the sample from Wales and Northern Ireland differ from the proportions in the population.

3.20   The results for this variable are illustrated in Figure 3.2. Generally, the highest scores were obtained by pupils in the South and the lowest by pupils in Wales.

3.21   Within England, mean scores of pupils in the South were higher than those in the North on all sub-categories, with the differences being significant on 9 of the 13 sub-categories. Mean scores of pupils in the South were higher than those in the Midlands on 12 of the sub-categories and significantly so on 3.

**Figure 3.2** *Differences from each sub-category's overall mean scaled score for region.*

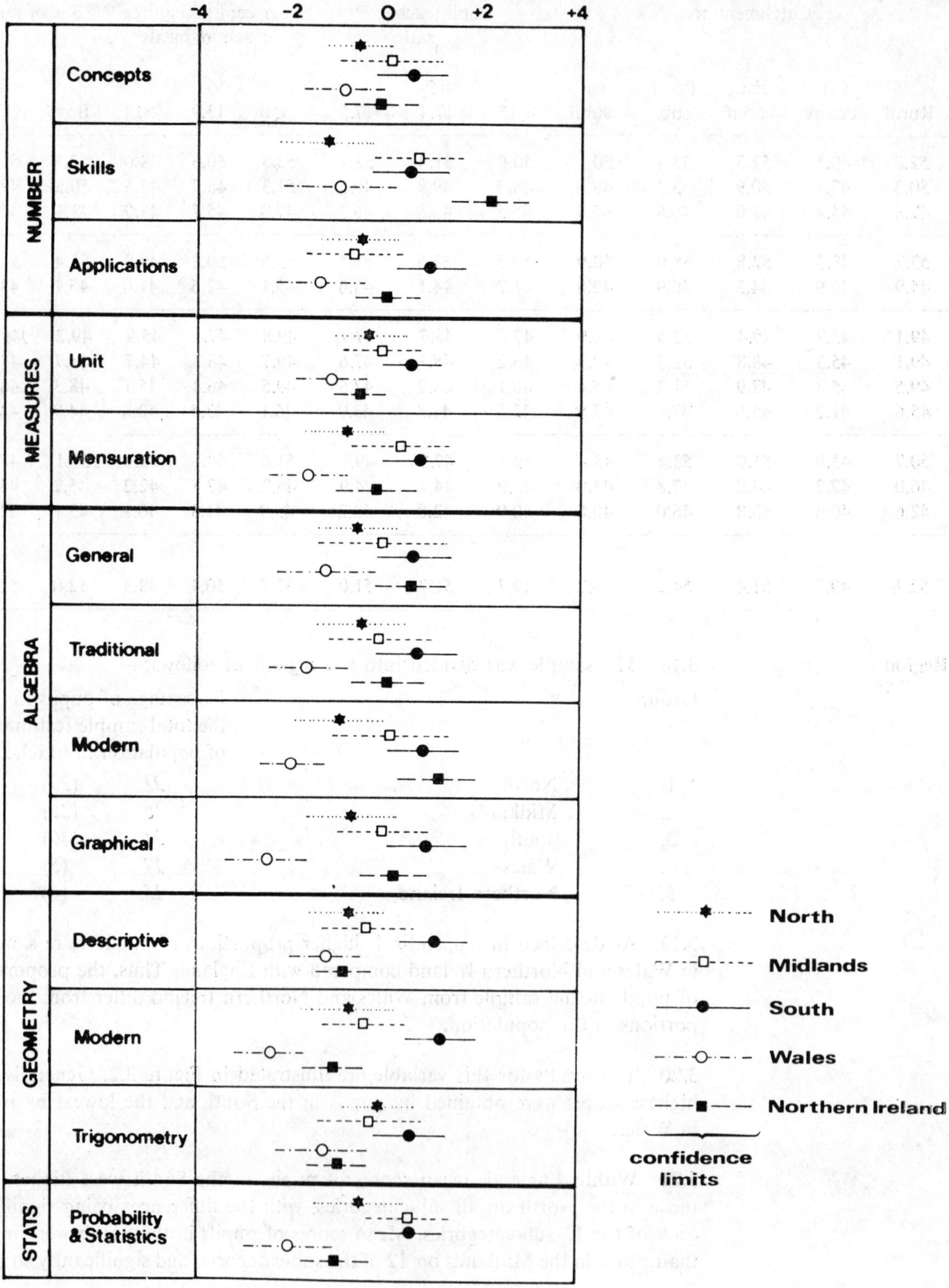

Legend:
- ·····★····· North
- ----□---- Midlands
- ——●—— South
- --○-- Wales
- ——■—— Northern Ireland

⎫ confidence limits

3.22   The differences between the mean scores of pupils in the Midlands and in the North were generally small, with only one of the 13 sub-categories on which the Midlands was higher, Number skills, reaching statistical significance.

3.23   Mean scores in Wales were the lowest of all five regions on all sub-categories except Number skills. Pupils in the South had mean scores which were significantly higher than those in Wales on all sub-categories; the Midlands were significantly higher than Wales on 7, Northern Ireland on 8 and the North on 3.

3.24   After pupils in the South, Northern Ireland tended to achieve the next highest scores. Although pupils in the South had higher mean scores than Northern Ireland on 11 sub-categories, only 5 of these differences were significant and, on Number Skills, pupils from Northern Ireland had significantly higher mean scores than those from the South. Mean scores in Northern Ireland were higher than those in the North on 8 sub-categories, with 3 of these differences being significant, while the differences between Northern Ireland and the Midlands were generally small.

**Location**

3.25   The sample was divided according to whether pupils were from a school in a non-metropolitan or metropolitan authority.

| Group | | Percentage of pupils in the total sample (estimate of population in brackets) | |
|---|---|---|---|
| 1. | Non-metropolitan | 75 | (65) |
| 2. | Metropolitan | 25 | (35) |

3.26   This classification of local education authorities is based on the nature of their whole area, so that some connurbations are not necessarily classified as metropolitan. The designation of authorities as either metropolitan or non-metropolitan is shown in Table A1.2. For the 1980 surveys more detailed information was collected on the area in which a school is situated and these results are reported in the section on catchment area.

3.27   As can be seen from Figure 3.3, scores of pupils from schools in non-metropolitan authorities were higher on all the sub-categories, with the differences being significant on all but two of them.

3.28   When location was analysed within region, non-metropolitan scores were found to be higher than metropolitan scores within each region, but these differences were largest in the Midlands and smallest in the North.

**Size of 15-plus age group**

3.29   This analysis relates only to schools in the maintained sample. This variable was analysed separately for England, Wales and Northern Ireland with different class intervals for the four classes of size of age group because of the different distributions of school size.

**Figure 3.3** *Differences from each sub-category's overall mean scaled score for location.*

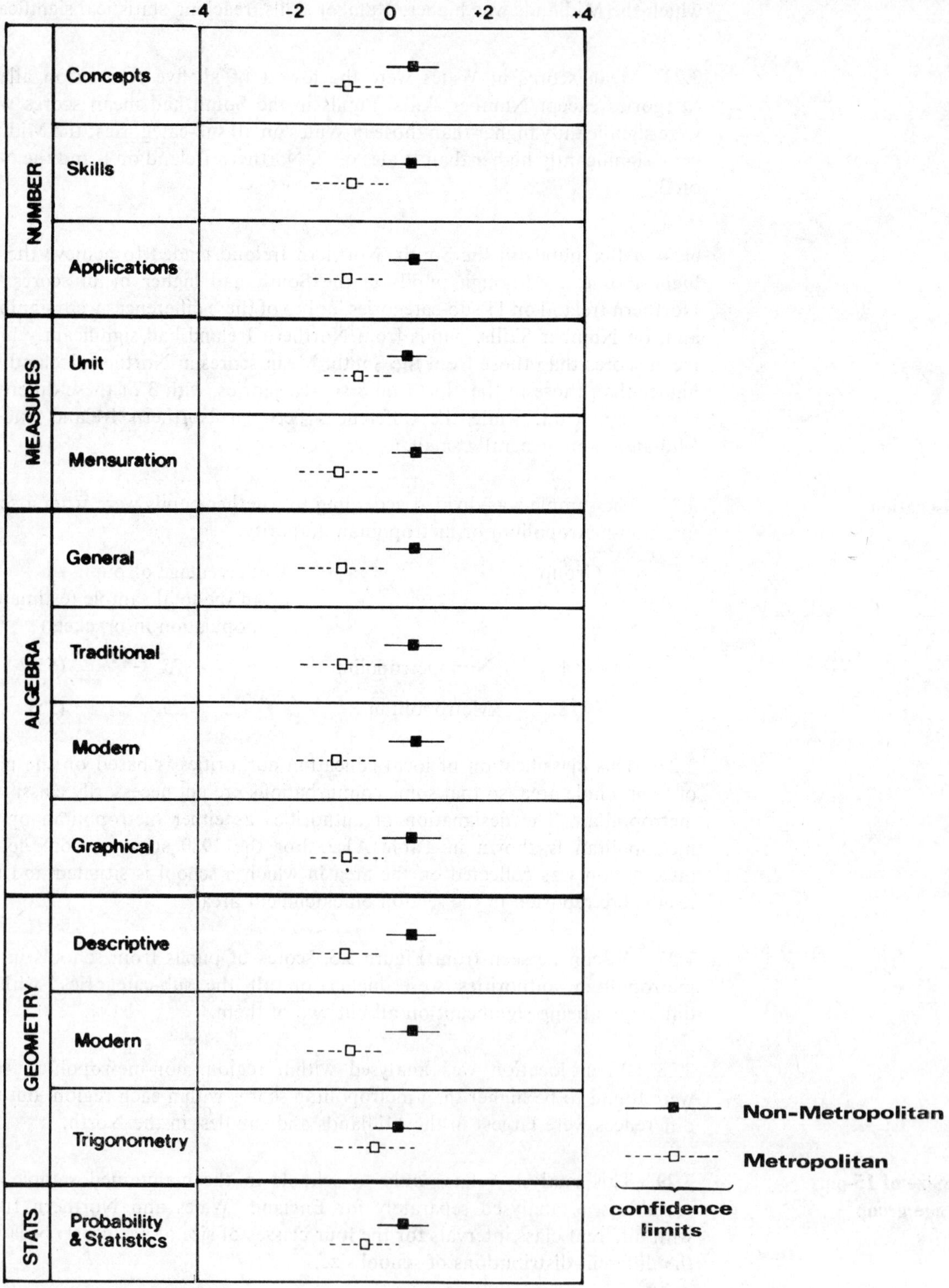

3.30  The results for England appear in Table 3.4, and the results for Wales and Northern Ireland are given in Tables 3.5 and 3.6.

3.31   In each of the three areas, the differences between the four categories of size of age group were small, so that there was no overall association between performance and size of 15-plus age group. Consequently, no further comment will be made on this variable, but it should be borne in mind, when looking at the tables of results, that none of the small differences which can be observed there is significant. Also, no graphs have been provided for this variable as the differences were too small for the graphs to be of any interest.

### ENGLAND

| Group | | Percentage of pupils in the maintained sample in England (estimate of population in brackets) | |
|---|---|---|---|
| 1. | 4–145 | *32* | *(17)* |
| 2. | 146–205 | *34* | *(31)* |
| 3. | 206–265 | *19* | *(24)* |
| 4. | 266+ | *15* | *(28)* |

### WALES

| Group | | Percentage of pupils in the maintained sample in Wales (estimate of population in brackets) | |
|---|---|---|---|
| 1. | 4–105 | *19* | *(9)* |
| 2. | 106–145 | *12* | *(7)* |
| 3. | 146–225 | *39* | *(36)* |
| 4. | 226+ | *30* | *(47)* |

**Table 3.5** *Mean scaled scores for each sub-category by size of 15-plus age group in Wales*

| | | 4–105 | 106–145 | 146–225 | 226+ |
|---|---|---|---|---|---|
| Number | Concepts | 51.4 | 51.4 | 51.0 | 51.0 |
| | Skills | 49.5 | 48.8 | 49.5 | 48.3 |
| | Applications | 45.8 | 46.2 | 45.2 | 45.4 |
| Measures | Unit | 51.6 | 49.3 | 51.3 | 51.1 |
| | Mensuration | 41.6 | 43.9 | 43.8 | 41.1 |
| Algebra | General | 47.9 | 46.9 | 48.3 | 46.7 |
| | Traditional | 47.7 | 49.2 | 46.3 | 46.1 |
| | Modern | 46.8 | 46.1 | 46.5 | 45.6 |
| | Graphical | 42.1 | 43.4 | 42.8 | 41.5 |
| Geometry | Descriptive | 49.0 | 48.8 | 48.2 | 48.9 |
| | Modern | 42.8 | 43.0 | 43.0 | 41.7 |
| | Trigonometry | 41.2 | 42.7 | 41.2 | 41.4 |
| Statistics | Statistics and probability | 49.6 | 50.3 | 49.1 | 49.4 |

NORTHERN IRELAND

| Group | | Percentage of pupils in the maintained sample of Northern Ireland (estimate of population in brackets) | |
|---|---|---|---|
| 1. | 4– 75 | 21 | (16) |
| 2. | 76–105 | 30 | (27) |
| 3. | 106–125 | 11 | (10) |
| 4. | 126+ | 38 | (47) |

**Table 3.6** *Mean scaled scores for each sub-category by size of 15-plus age group in Northern Ireland.*

| | | 4–75 | 76–105 | 106–125 | 126+ |
|---|---|---|---|---|---|
| Number | Concepts | 50.5 | 51.9 | 52.7 | 52.3 |
| | Skills | 52.2 | 53.2 | 52.0 | 51.7 |
| | Applications | 46.2 | 47.5 | 45.5 | 47.2 |
| Measures | Unit | 52.6 | 51.7 | 52.3 | 51.4 |
| | Mensuration | 43.8 | 44.6 | 44.3 | 43.5 |
| Algebra | General | 48.9 | 50.5 | 48.1 | 49.1 |
| | Traditional | 48.4 | 48.6 | 47.7 | 49.4 |
| | Modern | 48.6 | 49.8 | 47.9 | 49.4 |
| | Graphical | 45.9 | 45.3 | 42.9 | 44.8 |
| Geometry | Descriptive | 48.8 | 49.0 | 49.8 | 49.1 |
| | Modern | 43.5 | 45.1 | 42.1 | 43.5 |
| | Trigonometry | 41.0 | 41.7 | 40.5 | 42.4 |
| Statistics | Statistics and probability | 50.3 | 50.0 | 49.8 | 50.9 |

**School catchment area**

3.32 For this variable, each school was asked to indicate which category, from a list of five, best described the predominant nature of the area from which its pupils came. The relevant part of the pupil data form, completed by each school in the survey, is reproduced in Figure 3.4, describing in more detail each of the five categories of the school catchment area. Only a handful of the schools failed to answer the question or found all of the categories inappropriate. The same categories were used here as had been used in the HMI Secondary Survey[1] to describe schools' catchment areas.

[1]DES *Aspects of secondary education* HMSO, 1979.

**Figure 3.4** *Description of categories for school catchment area*

Which of the following best describes the catchment area of your school? Catchment area describes the environment from which pupils come, rather than the location of the school. If groups of pupils are drawn from more than one category of catchment area please select the predominant one.

(1)  Rural: few schools will have completely rural catchment areas, but some will draw their pupils from a mixture of farms, villages, small towns and/or small seaside resorts.

(2)  Areas subject to the problems associated with city centres. This covers schools in the middle of large cities drawing pupils from crowded and run-down property or from new flats and houses built to rehouse families on the old sites. It also covers overspill developments and some sections of new towns to which the problems associated with city centres have been exported.

(3)  Long established manufacturing areas. Socially, these areas would be relatively homogeneous: few pupils would come from very highly favoured groups, but very disadvantaged pupils would not present a notable problem.

(4)  Prosperous suburban. Mainly owner-occupied, but including the more prosperous council estates.

(5)  Less prosperous suburban. Mainly council estates. These areas would not suffer severely from social problems, but many pupils would have low motivation and aspirations.

| Group | | Percentage of pupils in the total sample (estimate of population in brackets) | |
|---|---|---|---|
| 1. | Rural | 26 | (23) |
| 2. | City centre | 13 | (16) |
| 3. | Established manufacturing area | 13 | (14) |
| 4. | Prosperous suburban | 23 | (23) |
| 5. | Less prosperous suburban | 22 | (24) |
| | Not given | 3 | (—) |

3.33   As can be seen from Figure 3.5, there was a wide variation of performance with this variable. The ordering of scores among the groups, which was highly consistent across the sub-categories, was, in decreasing order, prosperous suburban, rural, established manufacturing, less prosperous suburban and city centre. While pupils in group 4 scored significantly higher than group 1 on every sub-category, the differences between groups 1 and 3 were not so marked, with group 1 being higher than group 3 on 8 of the sub-categories but significantly so in only 2. Group 3 scored more highly than group 5 on every sub-category and this difference was significant in all but one—Modern geometry. Finally, pupils in group 5 scored higher than group 2 on 12 of the sub-categories, with 4 of those differences being significant. Thus, it can be seen that, in the ordering given above, the differences between the mean scores of pupils in prosperous suburban and rural tended to be quite large, as did those between established manufacturing and less prosperous suburban; those between less prosperous suburban and city centre were smaller, while the scores of rural were only marginally higher than those of established manufacturing.

3.34   When the catchment area variable was looked at within each of the regions, the same pattern of performance was found but the differences between the groupings in Wales were smaller than those in the other regions and generally not significant; the largest and generally significant differences were in Northern Ireland.

**Figure 3.5** *Differences from each sub-category's overall mean scaled score for school catchment area*

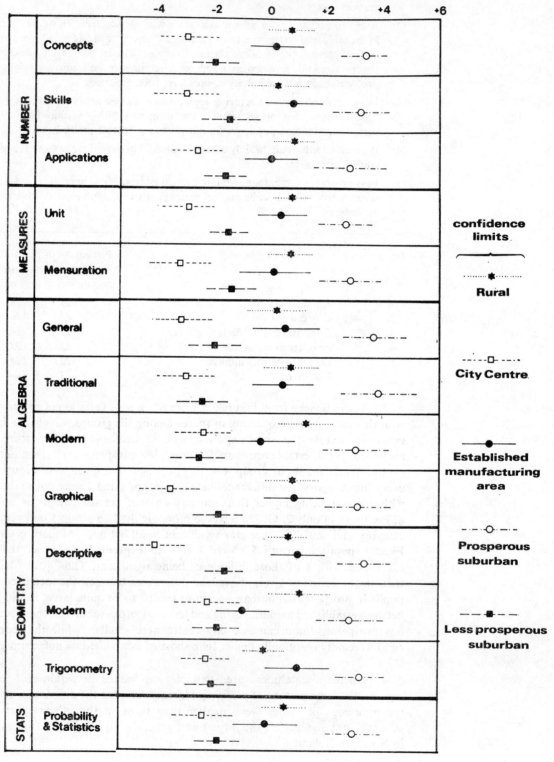

3.35   In connection with the location variable, it has already been mentioned that the classification of an authority as metropolitan or non-metropolitan may incorporate areas of different types. This means that the boundaries for the new catchment area variable do not exactly coincide with the metropolitan/non-metropolitan distinction. For instance, all the authorities in Wales and Northern Ireland are classified as non-metropolitan despite the high density of population in some areas. Thus, there were a few schools which, while being sited in non-metropolitan authorities, described themselves as being in city centres. However, the overall pattern for these two variables was consistent when they were looked at together. The group of non-metropolitan schools scored more highly no matter how they described their catchment area, although the difference between the non-metropolitan and metropolitan schools was least in the less prosperous suburban category and greatest in the rural and city centre categories.

3.36   There were some variations when the pupil/teacher ratio variable and the catchment area variable were looked at in terms of each other. The different association of the pupil/teacher ratio variable with performance in different catchment areas is described in the section on pupil/teacher ratio, but here it could be mentioned that the difference in performance between catchment areas was smaller in schools with a less favourable staffing ratio than in schools with a more favourable ratio.

**Pupil/teacher ratio**

3.37   This analysis relates only to schools in the maintained sample in England and Wales; data are not available for pupil/teacher ratio in Northern Ireland.

3.38   The pupils in the sample were allocated to one of three groups according to the pupil/teacher ratio of the school they attended.

| Group | | Percentage of pupils in the maintained sample in England and Wales (estimate of population in brackets) | |
|---|---|---|---|
| 1. | Ratio of less than 15 | *13* | *(14)* |
| 2. | Ratio between 15 and 17.4 | *63* | *(61)* |
| 3. | Ratio of 17.5 and over | *24* | *(25)* |

3.39   The results for this variable are illustrated in Figure 3.6. Scores of pupils from the middle group of schools were generally the highest, being higher than the first group on all sub-categories and higher than the third group on all but two. The differences between group 2 and group 1 were significant on 9 of the 13 sub-categories, while those between groups 2 and 3 were smaller and significant on only Unit measures. Group 3 mean scores were higher than group 1 on every sub-category and significantly so on 3 sub-categories.

3.40   Further investigation revealed that this pattern of performance was not consistent for schools in different areas. When pupil/teacher ratio was looked at in terms of the new catchment area variable it was found that the pattern of the overall sample (ie. scores to be ordered group 2, group 3 then group 1) occurred only in schools in prosperous suburban areas; in city centre schools scores increased with increasing pupil/teacher ratio (thus being ordered groups 3, 2 then 1) while for rural and established manufacturing area schools the opposite was the case—scores tended to decline with an increasing staffing ratio.

**Figure 3.6** *Differences from each sub-category's overall mean scaled score for pupil/teacher ratio.*

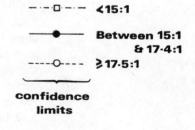

| | | |
|---|---|---|
| — · — □ — · — | | <15:1 |
| ———●——— | | Between 15:1 & 17·4:1 |
| ----○---- | | ≥17·5:1 |

confidence
limits

3.41 Figure 3.7 illustrates these variations with the scores obtained by each cell of the sample in the 2-way breakdown for the General algebra sub-category. The interaction of the two variables was significant beyond the 5 per cent level in five of the sub-categories. Figure 3.8 gives the percentage of the total sample in each cell.

**Figure 3.7** *Two-way breakdown of scaled scores for pupil/teacher ratio by school catchment area for general algebra.*

|  | Pupil/teacher ratio | | |
|---|---|---|---|
|  | 1 | 2 | 3 |
| Rural | 53.8 | 49.6 | 47.1 |
| City centre | 44.4 | 45.8 | 47.7 |
| Established manufacturing | 50.1 | 49.4 | 48.1 |
| Prosperous suburban | 50.0 | 52.1 | 48.6 |
| Less prosperous suburban | 47.6 | 46.3 | 47.7 |

**Figure 3.8** *Percentage of total maintained sample in England and Wales in each cell of the two-way breakdown of pupil/teacher ratio by school catchment area.*

|  | Pupil/teacher ratio | | |
|---|---|---|---|
|  | 1 | 2 | 3 |
| Rural | 1 | 14 | 8 |
| City centre | 5 | 9 | 3 |
| Established manufacturing | 2 | 10 | 4 |
| Prosperous suburban | 2 | 13 | 4 |
| Less prosperous suburban | 4 | 15 | 6 |

3.42 Similarly, when pupil/teacher ratio was analysed in terms of the location variable, within non-metropolitan areas scores were highest in group 2 schools, whereas in metropolitan areas scores increased with increasing pupil/teacher ratio. Also, the overall difference between non-metropolitan and metropolitan schools, noted in the section on location, occurred only in schools in groups 1 and 2; scores in schools within the highest pupil/teacher ratio group were similar in the two types of authorities and in fact were slightly higher in metropolitan authorities.

3.43 When looked at within region, it was found that there was no variation of performance with pupil/teacher ratio in the North; the pattern of the total sample was generally followed in the Midlands, the South and in Wales but the differences between the three pupil/teacher ratio groups of schools were greatest in the South.

3.44  It should be emphasised that the pupil/teacher variable is a school variable, not a pupil variable, and is obtained for each school by dividing the number of pupils in the school by the number of teachers on the staff. Clearly, this need bear little relation to the size of the mathematics group in which each pupil is being taught, since such factors as school organisation, a school's policy on remedial teaching, the presence of a sixth-form etc, all influence the deployment of teaching staff within a school. It is not clear from the analyses so far performed what the important factors influencing performance in relation to this variable are, but it is likely that there are various school characteristics underlying, and associated with, the pupil/teacher variable which would explain more fully the variation of performance reported in this section. It is intended to investigate these factors further, but it is clearly not an easy matter to disentangle the many individual practices of schools in order to discover a more general pattern influencing mathematics performance.

**Percentage of pupils taking free school meals**

3.45  This analysis relates only to schools in the maintained sample. The variable has been used as an indicator of the affluence of a school's catchment area. However, as a result of the 1980 Education Act, local education authorities are now permitted to fix their own criteria, above a statutory minimum, for entitlement to free school meals. This means that the free school meals variable is no longer a constant measure across the country. At the time of the survey there was a widely differing standard of eligibility for free school meals between different authorities and for this reason no attempt will be made to cross-tabulate this variable with others.

3.46  Schools were divided into three groups according to the number of pupils taking free school meals expressed as a percentage of the total number of pupils in the school.

| Group | | Percentage of pupils in the maintained sample (estimate of population in brackets) | |
|---|---|---|---|
| 1. | <6% taking free school meals | 43 | (50) |
| 2. | 6%–13.9% taking free school meals | 35 | (33) |
| 3. | ≥14% taking free school meals | 19 | (17) |
|  | Not given | 3 | (—) |

3.47  This method of calculating the free school meals provision differs from that used in previous surveys. In the past, the number of pupils taking free school meals was expressed as a percentage of those pupils taking school meals. The procedure has been changed due to a marked decline in the numbers of pupils taking school meals, whether free or purchased.

3.48  Despite these caveats, Figure 3.9 shows that there was a strong association between performance and this variable. Scores in group 1 were higher, and significantly so, than scores in group 2 in every sub-category. Scores in group 2 were higher than scores in group 3, again for every sub-category, with the differences being significant in 9 out of the 13 sub-categories.

**Figure 3.9**  *Differences from each sub-category's overall mean scaled score for free school meals*

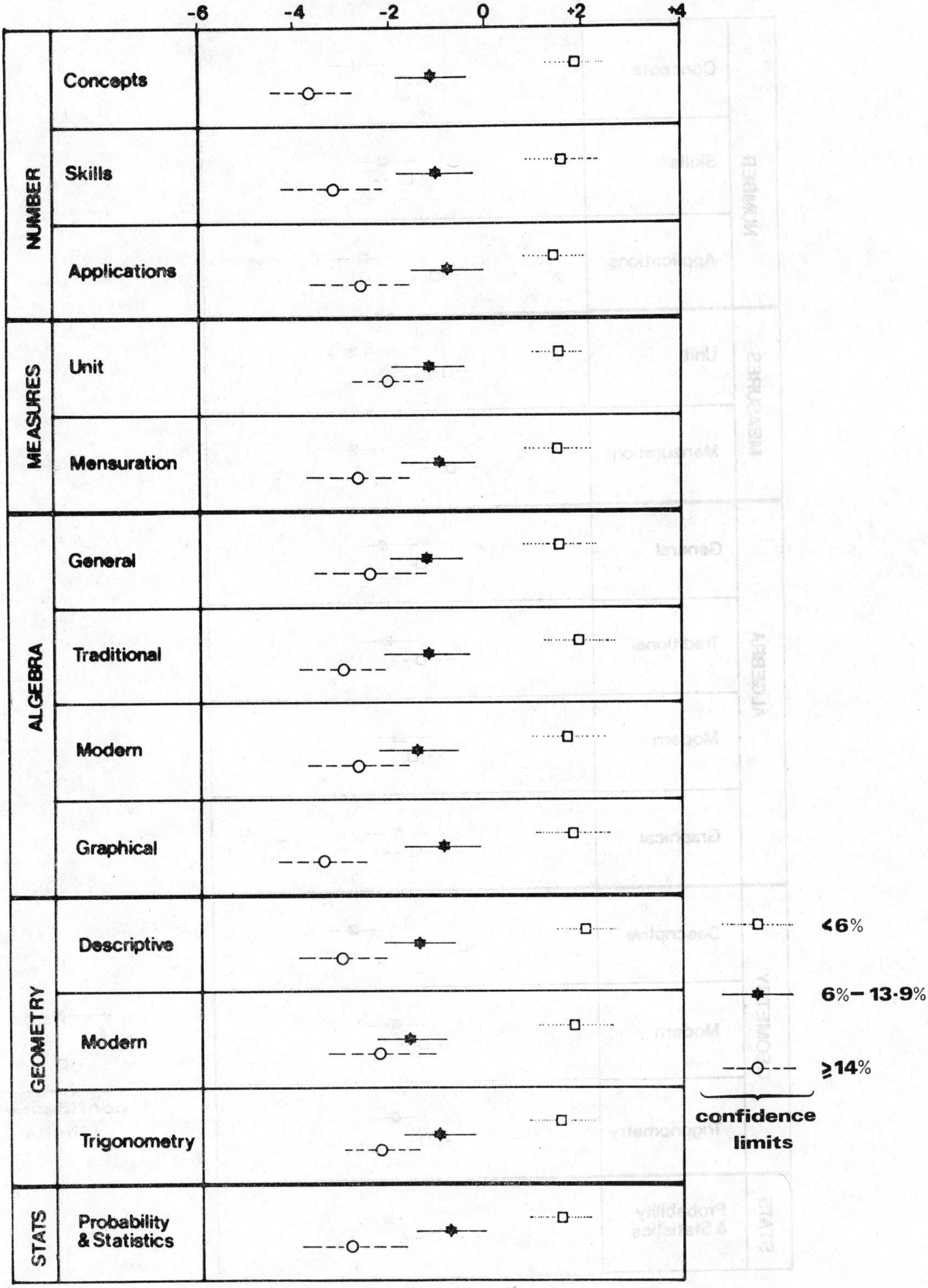

**Figure 3.10** *Differences from each sub-category's overall mean scaled score for sex of pupil.*

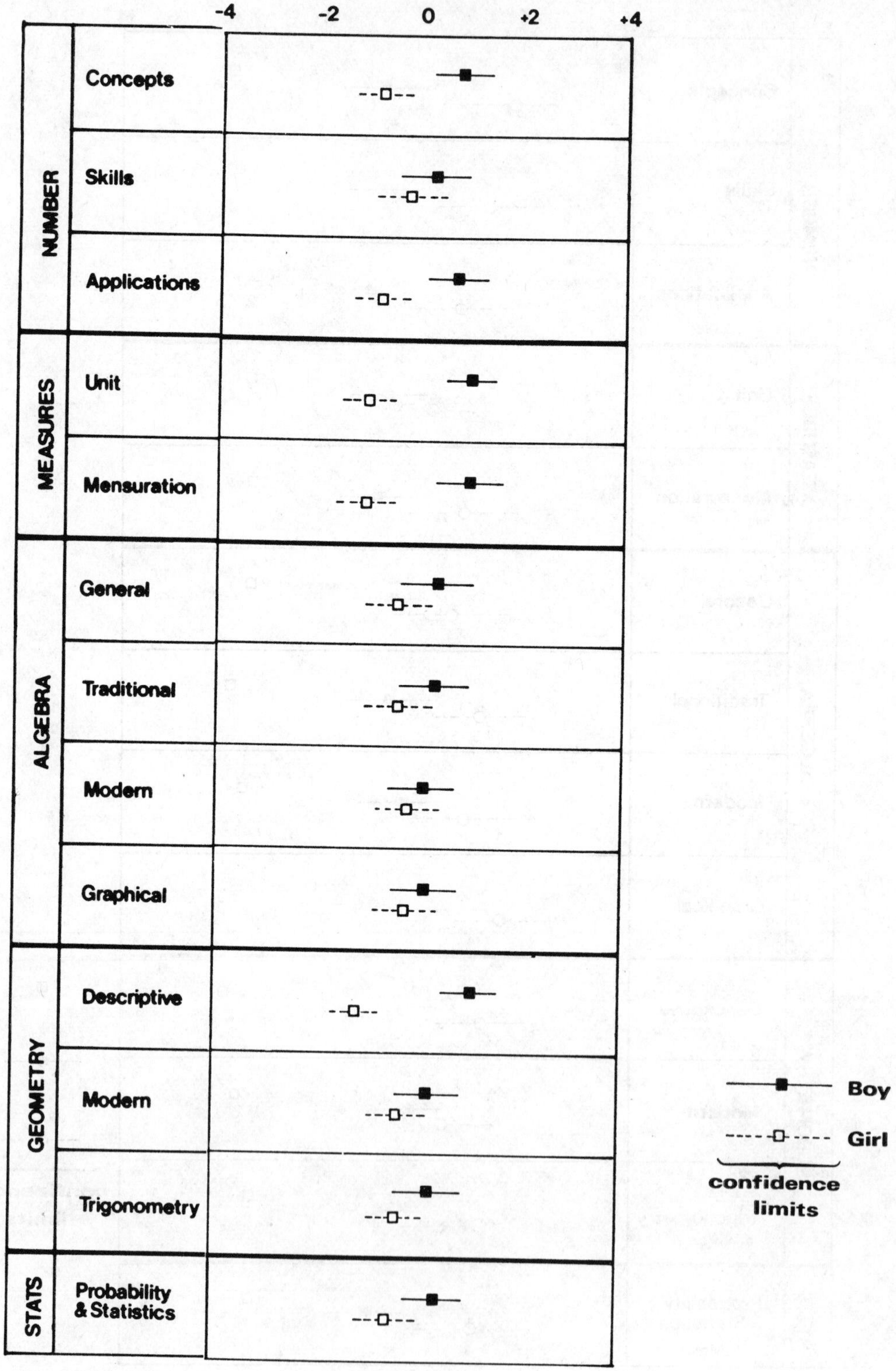

**Sex of pupil**

3.49   Separate scores were obtained for boys and girls on each sub-category and these are illustrated in Figure 3.10. Boys achieved higher scores on all of the sub-categories and these differences were significant on 6 of them. The differences were greatest on the two measures sub-categories and Descriptive geometry and least on Modern and Graphical algebra.

**Figure 3.11**   *Distribution of boys' and girls' scaled scores.*

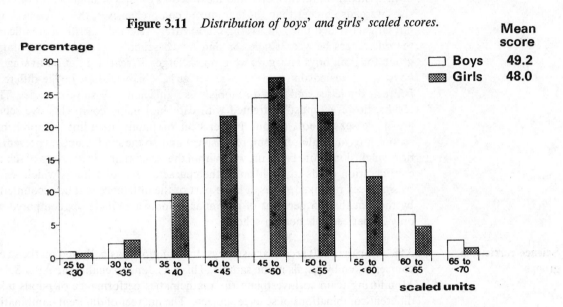

| | Mean score |
|---|---|
| ☐ Boys | 49.2 |
| ▦ Girls | 48.0 |

3.50   The distributions of boys' and girls' scores were investigated, using the scaled score of each pupil on the particular test they took. Figure 3.11 shows the distribution of boys' and girls' scores drawn using the same axes to aid comparison. From this it can be seen that the differences between the proportions of boys and girls in the top three score groups are larger than the differences in the bottom three groups. Thus, the higher mean scores of boys over girls are largely due to the greater preponderance of boys among the high scorers rather than girls among the low scorers. This is particularly clear when the proportions of boys and girls with scaled scores below 40 or above 60 are looked at:

| | Boys | Girls |
|---|---|---|
| Scores below 40 | *49%* | *51%* |
| Scores above 60 | *62%* | *38%* |

3.51   Boys' and girls' scores for the maintained sample were also analysed in terms of whether pupils attended mixed or single sex schools. Overall, both boys' and girls' mean scores were higher in single sex schools than in mixed schools in every sub-category. For boys, the differences were significant in all but one sub-category (Number applications) while for girls the differences were significant on 8 of the sub-categories.

3.52   Schools were than divided into two groups—comprehensives and other maintained (ie. grammar and modern schools)—and it was found that the differences between single sex and mixed schools were much greater within the other maintained group of schools than within comprehensives. While mean scores of boys in single sex comprehensive schools were higher than those of boys in mixed comprehensives and mean scores of girls in single sex comprehensives were also higher than those in mixed comprehensives, the differences were not large (1 scaled unit, on average) and rarely reached statistical significance; the differences between single sex and mixed schools in the 'other maintained' group for both boys and girls were much larger, 7 scaled units on average for boys and 6 scaled units on average for girls. This variation in the differences between single sex and mixed schools was significant in 9 sub-categories. These results, however, must be treated with care; not many comprehensive schools are single sex schools (about 15 per cent of pupils attending comprehensive schools are in single sex comprehensives) and so the small numbers prevent any firm conclusions from being drawn. Within the other maintained group of schools, consideration needs to be given to the characteristics of schools which tend to be single sex or mixed. Thus, a large part of the difference will be accounted for by the fact that 75 per cent of grammar schools are single sex compared with only 30 per cent of modern schools.

**Science curriculum groups**

3.53   For the 1980 secondary surveys, information was collected on the science courses taken by pupils in the sample. This was done to enable the APU Science Monitoring team to investigate the mathematics performance of pupils taking different combinations of science subjects. The number of different combinations of science subjects studied was very large, so the eleven most frequent combinations were used as separate curriculum groups, with the rest of the pupils being put together in the twelfth category.

| Group | Percentage of pupils in the total sample | Proportion of boys (%) | Proportion of girls (%) |
|---|---|---|---|
| 1. Biology | 14 | 19 | 81 |
| 2. Chemistry | 3 | 46 | 54 |
| 3. Physics | 8 | 88 | 12 |
| 4. Biology, chemistry | 5 | 28 | 72 |
| 5. Biology, physics | 4 | 63 | 37 |
| 6. Chemistry, physics | 7 | 83 | 17 |
| 7. Biology, chemistry, physics | 10 | 66 | 34 |
| 8. General science | 11 | 56 | 44 |
| 9. Human biology | 5 | 16 | 84 |
| 10. Another science course | 5 | 54 | 46 |
| 11. No science course | 11 | 35 | 65 |
| 12. Other | 17 | 59 | 41 |

3.54   There was a large variation of mean scores of pupils in these twelve groups, with those pupils taking all of biology, chemistry and physics and those taking chemistry and physics achieving the highest mean scores. Lowest mean scores tended to be achieved by pupils studying human biology and general science. The same information was collected for pupils taking part in the 1980 secondary language survey and it was found that the rank order of scores of the twelve curriculum groups was very similar for mathematics, reading and writing.

3.55 Within the twelve curriculum groups, separate mean scores for boys and girls were obtained and these showed a variable pattern of scores of boys relative to girls. For each sub-category, the mean score for girls was higher than the mean score for boys in about half of the curriculum groups. The three largest, and generally significant, differences where girls achieved higher mean scores than boys were for those pupils described as studying physics only, those studying biology and physics and those studying biology only. The only group in which boys' scores were significantly higher than girls' was the 'other' group but since this contained the largest number of pupils, this was enough to make the overall scores of boys higher. For those pupils studying one or more of biology, chemistry and physics, the results show either no significant difference between boys and girls or significantly higher mean scores for girls.

3.56 A variety of factors could be contributing to these results: girls who are good at mathematics may be more likely to opt to study science subjects after age 13; studying some science subjects may lead to higher mathematics scores for both sexes and compensates for, or precludes, some factors which otherwise negatively influence girls' mathematics performance; girls may do better at mathematics in schools with a strong science tradition; girls who opt to study science subjects may do so for more positive reasons than boys, because their choice is more unconventional and, as a result, are more highly motivated towards their school work. These factors are not mutually exclusive and it is not possible to determine which of them are contributing to the results presented here.

## Comparison with 1980 primary survey background variables

3.57 A similar set of variables was used to analyse the 1980 primary survey data, often with similar results. The results for location and sex of pupil were very similar to those obtained for the secondary survey. Thus, scores in non-metropolitan schools were consistently higher than those for metropolitan schools. Boys generally obtained higher scores at both age levels but the differences were smaller for the 11 year olds.

3.58 The categories used for the primary school locality variable were slightly different from those used for the secondary school catchment area variable, but a very similar trend emerged. Scores were highest in rural areas, rural-urban fringe and small towns and lowest in inner city areas, although the differences in scores were less for the primary survey than for the secondary.

3.59 In the primary survey, scores tended to increase with increasing pupil/teacher ratio, whereas at secondary level scores were highest for the middle ratio group. However, the greatest contrast in the results for the two surveys was for region.

3.60 At age 11, pupils in Northern Ireland achieved the highest scores on all but one sub-category, while those in Wales achieved the next highest scores in four of the five Number sub-categories. In some other sub-categories, mean Welsh scores were lower than those for pupils in both England and Northern Ireland. At the secondary level, scores of pupils in Northern Ireland were still amongst the highest but not by the substantial margin found in the primary survey. The greatest contrast, however, was in Wales. In the secondary survey, pupils in Wales achieved the lowest scores of the five regions on 12 of the 13 sub-categories (not Number skills), with many of the differences being significant. Thus, between the two age levels, pupils in Wales had changed from achieving scores around, and in some sub-categories above, the national average to achieving scores which were consistently below the national average.

## Conclusion

3.61 This and previous reports have commented on the association between performance and various background variables. The results for the variables common to all three surveys have been highly consistent but no conclusions can be drawn about causal relationships that there might be between these variables simply from any strong associations that have been found. It is clear from the analyses carried out so far that it is likely that there are other underlying factors which influence performance in mathematics. Although the pattern has been consistent, the variables so far used in the APU mathematics surveys have been very broad. More sensitive variables, deriving from more detailed information, would be required to give a fuller description of the factors affecting mathematics performance.

3.62 During the course of this series of five surveys, more information is being collected on certain school characteristics; and after five surveys it may be possible to amalgamate data across the years to make it feasible to consider smaller sub-sections of the samples. It is hoped that this will enable fuller descriptions of mathematics performance, and the factors affecting it, to be given in a retrospective report which will be written on the whole series of five surveys.

# 4 The written tests: item clusters

## Introduction

4.1   In the initial surveys, an attempt was made to classify each written test item in relation to its mathematical content (one of the sub-categories of the assessment framework) and the learning outcome it assessed (concept, skill or application). It was acknowledged in the first report that few items could be unequivocally classified in this way. Nearly all mathematics items involve both the understanding of concepts and the use of skills and most items have features relevant to several categories of the framework. Moreover, the extent to which each feature of one item influences the pattern of responses obtained from it is not often clear from an inspection of that item alone. More information can be derived from the results by comparing the response patterns of related items, particularly if they differ from each other by only a few, or even one, feature.

4.2   Thus, on page 78 the item *"What is the square root of 16?"* was answered correctly by 76 per cent of the pupils. This item involves a pupil's knowledge of the meaning of the words "square root" and the need to recall the result or how to work it out if it is not remembered. The requirement to find a square root is usually indicated symbolically; pupils in secondary schools could be expected to know both the name of the concept and the symbols which represent it. The four items on page 78 explore the influence of some of these features of the operation of finding a square root. These features include the size of the number involved and the various conventions for indicating that a square root is required.

4.3   By representing the results of clusters of items such as these, in particular by looking at characteristic errors and omission rates as well as success rates (facility), a comprehensive picture of the factors affecting pupils' performance on specific topics can be obtained. This picture can provide some insight into the nature of pupils' understanding of mathematics and the areas in which this understanding may be lacking.

4.4   Reporting on item clusters was introduced in the report on the 1979 survey and has been continued here. In some cases, very similar versions of the same item were used to investigate the effect of changing only one feature on the pattern of responses to an item, while keeping everything else constant. The sub-categories selected for more concentrated coverage are especially suitable for this approach, since the more times a sub-category appears in the tests, the more parallel versions of the same item can be included. In this connection, it should be borne in mind that parallel versions of the same item were always taken by different pupils; the test design was arranged so that all such items appeared in different tests.

4.5   The clusters reported in this chapter come from the sub-categories given greater emphasis in the 1980 survey. The same approach is being used in reporting the primary mathematics surveys and, where possible and appropriate, reference has been made here to the mathematical performance of 11 year olds on the same topic. In addition, two of the clusters, (Rotation, reflection and symmetry and Area and perimeter), contain items closely related to some of the topics used in the practical survey; mention of these has been made both in this chapter and in Chapter 2.

4.6   In all, the results of 62 items are reported in this chapter. These give details of the proportions of pupils answering each item correctly, the proportions making certain common errors and the proportions omitting the item. Nearly all of these items were used in the 1980 survey and some of them were included in all three surveys to date. In order to give a more complete picture of performance in some clusters, a few items have also been included which were used only in 1978 and 1979 but not in 1980. These items are marked with a dagger (†) after the item number. Acceptable responses are marked with an asterisk (*).

4.7   Some of the items reported here have also been used in the primary mathematics surveys. In these cases, the results for the 11 year olds are given in brackets underneath the results for the 15 year olds.

---

F1   What is the square root of 16?        .................

| Response | ±4* +4 and —4 | 4* | 8 | Other | Omitted |
|---|---|---|---|---|---|
| | 2% | 74% | 4% | 11% | 9% |

---

F2        $\sqrt{16} =$ .................

| Response | ±4* +4 and —4 | 4* | 8 | Other | Omitted |
|---|---|---|---|---|---|
| | 2% | 69% | 3% | 10% | 16% |

---

F3        $16^{\frac{1}{2}} =$ .................

| Response | ±4* +4 and —4 | 4* | 8 | 16.5 | Other | Omitted |
|---|---|---|---|---|---|---|
| | 0% | 14% | 30% | 14% | 22% | 20% |

---

F4   Ring the number which is nearest to $\sqrt{200}$

| 14* | 100 | 45 | 20 | 72 | Omitted |
|---|---|---|---|---|---|
| 50% | 25% | 4% | 16% | 1% | 4% |

4.8   The items are numbered sequentially through three sections–Numbers Measures and Geometry. The letter preceding each number is the code letter for the sub-category in which the item was placed, as follows:—

| | |
|---|---|
| F | Number concepts |
| H | Number skills |
| J | Number applications |
| R | Unit measures |
| Q | Mensuration |
| P | Descriptive geometry. |

4.9   All the items presented here appeared in two tests and each percentage quoted is the average of the two results for an item.

## The item clusters

**Number**

*Powers and roots*

4.10   This cluster relates to the different ways of writing powers and roots of numbers and also to the relative sizes of numbers to various powers.

4.11   The first four items, F1 to F4, all concern the idea of the square root of a number. The first three use a small number, in the belief that most pupils will be familiar with the fact that four 4's are sixteen. The highest facility occurs in F1, where the words 'square root' actually appear in the item, with 76 per cent of the pupils being successful. Nearly as many though, 71 per cent, were successful in F2 where the root symbol was used instead. In item F3, the question was set using index notation, and the omission rate of 20 per cent suggests that fewer pupils were familiar with this notation than with the root sign. It can also be seen that, in all three items, very few of the pupils gave both square roots. On being confronted with the index notation in F3, many pupils resorted to incorrect methods. The most common of these was to halve 16, or to use the index as a multiplier, to obtain the answer 8. While this answer was given by a few pupils in both F1 and 2, the incidence of it rose substantially to 30 per cent in F3. Another common misinterpretation of the question was to take it as $16\frac{1}{2}$ and rewrite this as a decimal, getting 16.5; this was done by 14 per cent of the pupils. It was noted in the second secondary survey report that there was a tendency for between 10 and 20 per cent of pupils to treat a whole number index as a multiplier and it can be seen here that this tendency is even stronger with a fractional index. In the second primary survey report it was noted that nearly 50 per cent of 11 year old pupils also treated a whole number index as a multiplying factor, about four times as many as added the index to the base number. Item F4 tested understanding of the square root operation in a rather different way. The number was much larger, was not a perfect square and a multiple choice format was used to keep the computational load to a minimum. The facility obtained was 50 per cent, some 20 per cent lower than F2 where the square root symbol was also used. It is interesting to note the relatively high number of pupils who selected 100, that is, taking the square root symbol as halving. In F2, only 2 per cent of the pupils adopted this strategy when the number was small and a perfect square, while in F4 a quarter of the pupils thought that this was the correct interpretation of the symbol.

The other commonly selected alternative was the answer 20, chosen by 16 per cent of the pupils, possibly either because its digits were closest to those in 200 or because the root sign was interpreted as a division by 10.

---

F5   Which of these numbers is the largest?

| | | |
|---|---|---|
| *A. | $10^3$ | 78% |
| B. | $10^{-4}$ | 9% |
| C. | $10^{-1}$ | 0% |
| D. | $10^2$ | 2% |
| E. | 10 | 7% |
| Omitted | | 4% |

---

F6   Which of these numbers is the largest?

| | | |
|---|---|---|
| *A. | $2^3$ | 72% |
| B. | $2^{-4}$ | 12% |
| C. | $2^{-1}$ | 1% |
| D. | $2^2$ | 2% |
| E. | 2 | 10% |
| Omitted | | 3% |

---

F7   Which of these numbers is the smallest

| | | |
|---|---|---|
| A. | $10^3$ | 2% |
| *B | $10^{-4}$ | 68% |
| C. | $10^{-1}$ | 10% |
| D. | $10^2$ | 0% |
| E. | 10 | 17% |
| Omitted | | 3% |

---

F8   $4^3 = $ ..................

| Response | 64* | 16 | 12 | Other | Omitted |
|---|---|---|---|---|---|
| | 57% | 2% | 12% | 15% | 14% |

---

F9   What is the cube of 4?

| Response | 64* | 16 | 12 | 256 | 2 | Other | Omitted |
|---|---|---|---|---|---|---|---|
| | 34% | 15% | 3% | 6% | 8% | 21% | 13% |

4.12   The three items, F5 to F7, required pupils to give the largest or smallest of five numbers, expressed as the same powers of either 10 or 2. Selecting the largest proved somewhat easier, with 78 per cent selecting the correct power of 10 in F5, and only slightly fewer (72 per cent) being successful in F6; the difference presumably being due to a few pupils being put off by the more unusual use of

2 as the base of a power. The pattern of selection of the other alternatives was similar in these two items; around 10 per cent selected the second alternative, which contains the highest digit, thus ignoring the negative sign and around 10 per cent thought that the largest number was the one alternative with no power at all. When asked to give the smallest number in F7, the success rate was slightly lower at 68 per cent. Here, the next most frequently selected alternative was the one with no power; thus, in all three items, the alternative with no power (which is in fact the middle number in order of size) was a common wrong choice, being given by around 10 per cent of the pupils as the largest number and by 17 per cent as the smallest number.

4.13  Items F8 and F9 were on the operation of cubing a number. In F8, the question was given using an index of 3 and the facility was 57 per cent with 12 per cent using the index as a multiplier. In F9, the term 'cube' was used instead of the index with a considerably lower facility of 34 per cent. The answer 12 was still given in this item, but by fewer pupils (only 3 per cent). In F9, 15 per cent of the pupils give the square of 4 instead of the cube, but in F8, set in index form, this answer was much rarer, being given by only 2 per cent of the pupils. The situation here could be considered similar to that in F3. It seems that both items use a format of which pupils have limited experience; a fractional index in F3 and an unfamiliar term in F9, but in both cases such pupils resorted to a more common operation.

4.14  Two items on index notation were reported on in the second secondary survey report. In one, pupils were asked for the value of $10^2$, and, in the other, for the value of $y^3$ when $y = 3$. The success rate for $10^2$ was higher, at 73 per cent, than for $4^3$, with 10 per cent giving the answer 20, which was the multiplicative strategy. For $y^3$, 44 per cent gave the correct answer, with 16 per cent giving the answer 9.

4.15  From this it can be seen that an index of 2 is associated with a higher success rate than an index of 3, while the proportion using the index as a multiplying factor is very similar in the numerical items using indices 2 and 3, but slightly higher in the algebraic item using index 3. When a square root was expressed as an index, there was a much stronger tendency to treat the index as a multiplier, while, when the root sign or the term itself was used, only a few pupils adopted the strategy of halving.

4.16  It is clear that between 10 per cent and 25 per cent of pupils use an index as a multiplier. The actual proportion doing so depends on factors such as the size of the number being raised to a power, whether algebraic symbols are involved, and presentational aspects of items.

*Division*

4.17  This small group of items investigated the effects of representing exactly the same, reasonably easy, division in different ways. The easiest of these, with a facility of 87 per cent, was J10 where the question was set in verbal form, using the idea of sharing 112p among 7 people. The facility was nearly as high in the next two, H11 and F12, with one using a division sign and the other set in verbal form. The formats used in H13 and F14, however, did result in lower facilities. H13 used a ratio presentation and obtained a facility of 71 per cent, while on F14, set in verbal form using 1/7, the facility was again lower at 61 per cent. The decline in the facility of these last two items is partly due to an increase in the omission rate. Very few pupils omitted the first three items, but the ratio form of H13 was omitted by 12 per cent of the pupils and the verbal fraction form of F14 by 22 per cent. The 'Other' incorrect responses in H13 were looked at in more detail to discover what other incorrect strategies were adopted by pupils. The number of pupils giving a particular response was usually very small, but there were certain categories of incorrect answer, where pupils often realised that they had to divide, but then made computational errors. One was to obtain the wrong remainder at the first step of dividing 7 into 11 (e.g. '7 goes into 11 once remainder 3)', another to get 17 instead of 16 (possibly by getting the 6 and 7 in their product of 42 confused). Finally, there were some pupils who attempted the item by cancelling, correctly getting 16 as the numerator but leaving 7 in the denominator, thus giving 16/7 instead of 16/1.

4.18   A cluster of primary items on division was described in the report of the 1980 primary survey. A much larger collection of items was used to investigate the effects of different numbers as well as of different presentations, and a similar influence of presentation was found. While around 80 per cent of 11 year olds were successful on $84 \div 4$, a slightly easier division than in this cluster, the same item in ratio form ($\frac{84}{4}$) produced a success rate some 30 per cent lower.

---

J10   112p is to be shared equally among 7 people.

How much does each person get?

.................p

| Response | 16* | Other | Omitted |
|----------|-----|-------|---------|
| | 87% | 11% | 2% |

---

H11      $112 \div 7 =$ ......................

| Response | 16* | Other | Omitted |
|----------|-----|-------|---------|
| | 84% | 12% | 4% |

---

F12   How many 7's are there in 112? .....................

| Response | 16* | 784 | Other | Omitted |
|----------|-----|-----|-------|---------|
| | 83% | 1% | 13% | 3% |

---

H13      $\frac{112}{7} =$ ...............................

| Response | 16* | Other | Omitted |
|----------|-----|-------|---------|
| | 71% | 17% | 12% |

---

F14   What is $\frac{1}{7}$ of 112?   ......................

| Response | 16* | Other | Omitted |
|---|---|---|---|
| | *61%* | *17%* | *22%* |

4.19   Thus, for 11 year olds, a division set in ratio form lowered the facility of an item much more than for 15 year olds. Also, comparing the omit rates in items H11 and H13, the omit rate increased from 4 per cent to 12 per cent while for the 11 year olds the omit rate increased from 7 per cent to 27 per cent.

**Measures**

*Area and perimeter*

4.20   Items discussed in this section tested the idea of covering shapes with units of area of varying types as well as the method of calculating area from given linear dimensions. There were also a few items on finding perimeters in which a certain amount of confusion between area and perimeter was evident.

4.21   The group of items R1 to R5 are all concerned with the area of a rectangle 4 cm by 3 cm. In none of these items is the term 'area' used; instead they all ask directly for the number of the given unit required to cover the rectangle. The easiest of these, not surprisingly, is R1 where the number of 1 cm squares which will fit into the rectangle was asked for. 86 per cent of the pupils answered this item correctly while, more interestingly, about the same number, 84 per cent, were correct on the same item set without a diagram (R2). Thus, the diagram provided in R1 seems to be of no assistance to pupils. Items R3 to R5 involve non-standard units of area; in R3, while the unit of area is a half-square, the rectangle itself is divided into 1 cm squares with the result that the facility is still high at 87 per cent. A further 6 per cent, however, did not take account of the unit of area being used and gave the answer 12, the number of grid squares in the rectangle. In items R4 and R5 the use of a non-standard unit of area, a half-centimetre square, did lower the success rate considerably; for the dimensions being given as both $\frac{1}{2}$ cm and 0.5 cm, the facility was 59 per cent. However, the two different ways of specifying the dimensions

R1

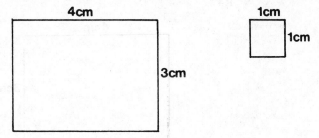

How many of the squares will fit into the rectangle?

......................

| Response: | 12* | 7 | 14 | Other | Omitted |
|---|---|---|---|---|---|
| | *86%* | *1%* | *<1%* | *11%* | *2%* |
| *(1980 primary* | *72%* | *NC* | *4%* | *22%* | *2%)* |
| | *NC = Not coded* | | | | |

R2

How many squares, 1 cm by 1 cm, will fit into a
rectangle 4 cm by 3 cm?

.....................

| Response | 12* | 7 | 24 | Other | Omitted |
|----------|-----|-----|-----|-------|---------|
| | 84% | 1% | 8% | 5% | 2% |

R3

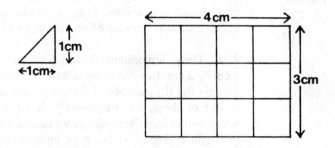

How many of the triangles fit into the rectangle?

.....................

| Response | 24* | 12 | Other | Omitted |
|----------|-----|-----|-------|---------|
| | 87% | 6% | 6% | 1% |
| (1980 primary | 72% | 11% | 12% | 5%) |

R4

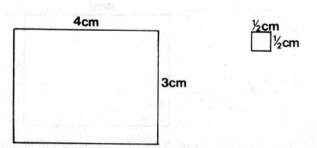

How many of the squares will fit into the rectangle?

.....................

| Response | 48* | 24 | 12 | Other | Omitted |
|----------|-----|-----|-----|-------|---------|
| | 59% | 15% | 5% | 18% | 3% |

R5

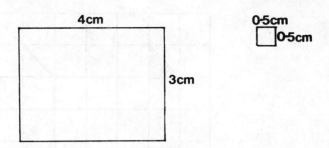

How many of the squares will fit into the rectangle?

........................

| Response | 48* | 24 | 12 | Other | Omitted |
|---|---|---|---|---|---|
| | 59% | 10% | 3% | 24% | 4% |

R6

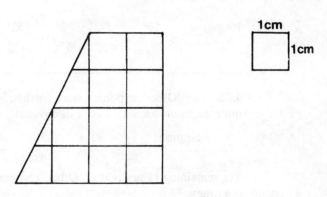

What is the area of this figure?

........................ cm²

| Response | 12* | 14 | 10 | 11 | Other | Omitted |
|---|---|---|---|---|---|---|
| | 76% | 1% | 3% | 2% | 14% | 4% |
| (1980 primary | 59% | 3% | 7% | 3% | 22% | 6%) |

were associated with different frequencies of incorrect response. In R4, where ½ cm was used, 15 per cent of the pupils doubled the area of the rectangle in square centimetres to get 24, while 5 per cent took no account of the different unit and gave 12. When the dimension was given as 0.5 cm, the incidence of both of these errors declined; fewer pupils, 10 per cent rather than 15 per cent, doubled 12 to get 24 and the tendency to take no account of the different unit was also slightly less.

R7    In the diagram the shaded triangle represents a unit of area.

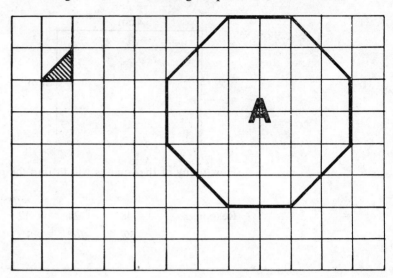

How many such units are there in shape A?

.........................

| Response | 56* | 28 | 8 | 52 | 55 | 32 | Other | Omitted |
|---|---|---|---|---|---|---|---|---|
| | 70% | 4% | 6% | 3% | 3% | 2% | 11% | 1% |

4.22   The 'Other responses were further investigated in R5 and a few more quite common responses were discovered:

| Response: | 30 | 35 | 40 | 42 | 56 |
|---|---|---|---|---|---|
| | 2% | 3% | 2% | 3% | 1% |

The remaining 11 per cent of 'Other' responses were errors made less frequently than these.

4.23   It is largely conjecture to supply explanations of these errors, but one which could be offered here is for 35: 35 can be obtained by adding the dimensions of the rectangle to get seven and multiplying by the 5 in the square unit. Despite the presence of a decimal (0.5) in the question, there were no decimal answers to this item.

4.24   The facility of item R6 was slightly lower than for items R1 to R3. Like items R1 and R2, the unit given is a 1 cm square and like R3 there is a grid drawn on the shape, but, unlike the previous items, it is a less regular shape than a rectangle and the term 'area' is used in the question. The combination of these features, the first two of which might be expected to make the item easier than R1 to R3 and the last two more difficult, resulted in a facility of 76 per cent, some 10 per cent lower than R1 to R3.

4.25   Items R7 and R8 involve both non-standard units of area and a more complex shape, although some assistance is provided by the grid drawn on the shape. Despite the different units of area given in each item, the facilities of the two are similar at around 70 per cent. A common wrong answer was 8 in R7 and 4 in R8, both given by around 6 per cent of the pupils.

R8    In the diagram the shaded triangle represents a unit of area.

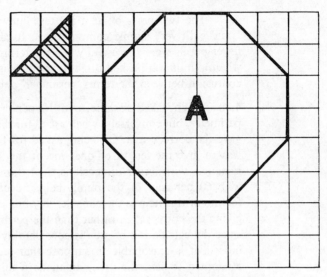

How many such units are there in shape A?

......................

| Response | 14* | 9 | 28 | 4 | Other | Omitted |
|---|---|---|---|---|---|---|
| | 69% | 1% | 7% | 7% | 15% | 1% |

R9

**3 cm**

What is the perimeter of this square?    (i)                cm
......................

What is the area of the square?    (ii)                cm²
......................

| (i) Response | 12* | 6 | 3 | 9 | Other | Omitted |
|---|---|---|---|---|---|---|
| | 74% | 3% | 8% | 3% | 8% | 4% |
| (1980 primary | 68% | NC | 11% | 4% | 10% | 7%) |
| (ii) Response | 9* | 6 | 3 | 12 | Other | Omitted |
| | 71% | 4% | 3% | 10% | 10% | 2% |
| (1980 primary | 46% | NC | 7% | 20% | 19% | 8%) |

4.26   These are the answers which would be obtained by counting up the actual number of triangles present in the figures which are the same size as the given units, there being 8 around the outside in R7 and 4 in R8. The area of the shape in square units, 28, is also given in both items, by 4 per cent in R7 and 7 per cent in R8.

4.27   The two parts of item R9 test knowledge of the terms 'perimeter' and 'area' with very simple computations. It can be seen that around 15 per cent fewer pupils were successful when the term 'area' was used than in R1 and R2 where pupils were asked directly about 1 cm squares. R9 also illustrates some confusion between the terms 'perimeter' and 'area'.

4.28   When asked for the area 10 per cent of the pupils gave the correct perimeter, but conversely, when asked for the perimeter fewer pupils, 3 per cent, gave the correct area. On being asked for the perimeter a more frequent error was to give the length of one side of the square. In R10, the perimeter of a rectangle with larger dimensions than those of previous items was asked for, with 60 per cent of the pupils being successful. However, the most striking feature of this item is the considerably higher proportion of pupils, 19 per cent, giving the correct area rather than the perimeter. This is particularly surprising since the calculation of area is considerably harder than finding the perimeter; indeed, it is reasonable to suppose that more than 19 per cent of the pupils attempted to find the area but made a mistake with the multiplication. The explanation for the increase in this error, in response to this item, may lie in its presentation. It is possible that some pupils are used to seeing this type of presentation in area questions and so assumed that this was also one of them.

4.29   Items R11 to R14 are all concerned with changing the dimensions of rectangles, but preserving their area. The first three involve the same two rectangles in different contexts. In the easiest of these, R11, a grid is provided on which to draw the new rectangle so that only counting is necessary to obtain the correct answer. 76 per cent of the pupils answered this correctly, with only 2 per cent drawing a rectangle 6 by 5 units, which is the answer

R10

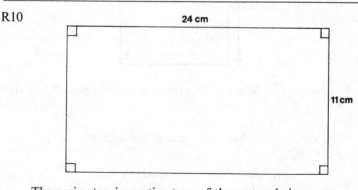

The perimeter, in centimetres, of the rectangle is

............................ cm

| Response | 70* | 35 | 264 | Other | Omitted |
|----------|-----|-----|-----|-------|---------|
| | 60% | 4% | 19% | 14% | 3% |

R11  Using the line XY as base, draw a rectangle which has the same area as shape A.

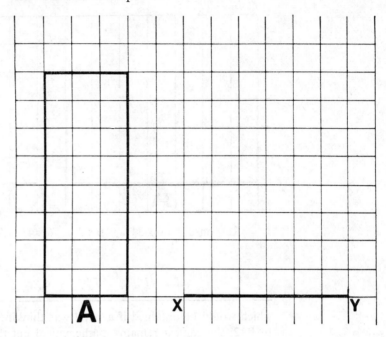

| Response | 6 x 4* | 6 x 5 | Same rectangle but different orientation | Other | Omitted |
|---|---|---|---|---|---|
| | 76% | 2% | 5% | 14% | 3% |

R12  A rectangle has length 8m and width 3m. Another rectangle of the same area is drawn with length 6m. What is its width?

.......................... m

| Response | 4* | 5 | 3 | Other | Omitted |
|---|---|---|---|---|---|
| | 60% | 11% | 2% | 22% | 5% |

R13  A gardener has enough grass-seed to seed a lawn 8m by 3m. If, instead, he uses it to seed a lawn 6m long, how wide will it be?

.......................... m

| Response | 4* | 5 | 3 | Other | Omitted |
|---|---|---|---|---|---|
| | 51% | 24% | 1% | 16% | 8% |

R14   Using the line XY as base, draw a rectangle which has the same area as shape A.

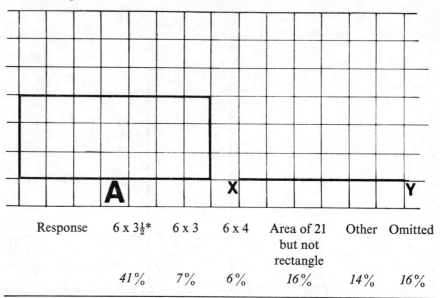

| Response | 6 x 3½* | 6 x 3 | 6 x 4 | Area of 21 but not rectangle | Other | Omitted |
|---|---|---|---|---|---|---|
| | 41% | 7% | 6% | 16% | 14% | 16% |

which would be obtained if a pupil was thinking of preserving the perimeter. In R12, the context remains mathematical but the problem is set in a purely verbal form with a consequently lower facility of 60 per cent. Also, the proportion preserving perimeter and giving the answer 5 increased to 11 per cent. R13 set the same problem in a more practical context which resulted in a further decline in facility to 51 per cent. As well as a reduction in facility, the practical context induced more pupils to consider that the correct procedure was to obtain a rectangle with the same perimeter – the 24 per cent giving the answer 5 is more than twice the proportion in R12. It could be mentioned here that in the Area topic in the practical survey, a small proportion of pupils, 7 per cent, when describing how to find the area of an irregular shape, believed that shapes with the same perimeter did in fact have the same area (see paragraph 2.39).

4.30   R14 used the same idea as R11, but this time one of the dimensions of the answer was not an integral number. The facility of this item was lower, at 41 per cent, but a further 16 per cent drew a figure of area 21 without following the instruction to draw a rectangle. Again, some pupils, 6 per cent, preserved the perimeter rather than the area and drew a rectangle 6 by 4.

4.31   The last three items considered here involved comparisons of areas and lengths. In R15, 84 per cent of the pupils selected the alternative stating that the area had been preserved. However, in R16, 43 per cent thought that the perimeter of the shape would be preserved, with 39 per cent selecting the correct option. In R17, pupils were asked to select all the correct statements relating to comparisons made between three lines, A, B and C. Two of the five statements were true and 38 per cent of the pupils selected these two together. However, 38 per cent selected statements 1 and 3, indicating that while they correctly realised that line C was longer than line A they also thought, incorrectly, that lines A and B were equal in length. A further 12 per cent, by selecting statements

R15 I cut a square X into 2 pieces and arrange the pieces to make a new shape Y like this:

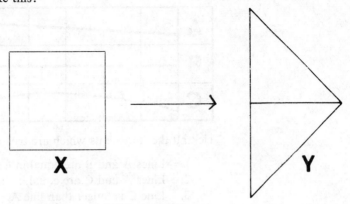

Which of these statements about X and Y is true?

    A. X has the bigger area.
    B. Y has the bigger area.
    C. X and Y have the same area.
    D. You cannot tell if one area is bigger or not.

| Response: | A | B | C* | D | Other | Omitted |
|---|---|---|---|---|---|---|
| | 3% | 7% | 84% | 4% | 1% | 1% |

R16 I cut a square X into 2 pieces and arrange the pieces to make a new shape Y like this:

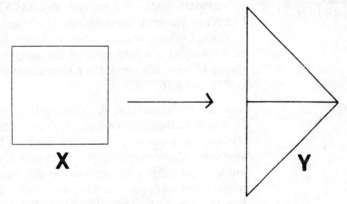

Which of these statements about X and Y is true?

    A. X has the bigger perimeter.
    B. Y has the bigger perimeter.
    C. X and Y have the same perimeter.
    D. You cannot tell if one perimeter is bigger or not.

| Response: | A | B* | C | D | Other | Omitted |
|---|---|---|---|---|---|---|
| | 4% | 39% | 43% | 8% | 3% | 3% |

R17

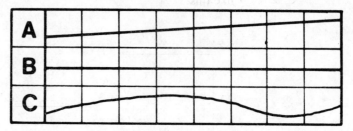

Tick all the statements which are true about lines A, B and C.

1. Lines A and B are equal in length.
2. Lines A and C are equal in length.
3. Line C is longer than line A.
4. Line A is longer than line C.
5. Line A is longer than line B.

| Statements ticked: | 3 & 5* | 1 & 3 | 1 & 2 | 1 & any others | 3 only | Other | Omitted |
|---|---|---|---|---|---|---|---|
| | 38% | 38% | 12% | 3% | 2% | 6% | 1% |

1 and 2, considered that all three lines were equal. In fact, a total of 53 per cent of the pupils, by selecting at least statement 1, thought that lines A and B were equal in length.

[1]Hart, K. M. (Ed) (1981) *Children's understanding of mathematics 11–16*, John Murray.

4.32   Item R17 was similar to, but more difficult than, one used by the Concepts in Secondary Maths and Science project (CSMS)[1] with 12, 13 and 14 year olds. There was the same considerable confusion over the relative lengths of lines on a grid. Evidence from interviews with pupils suggested that those who thought the lines equal in length counted the squares. CSMS had also found confusion among 14 year olds about the conservation of area and perimeter in items such as R15 and R16.

[1]*Mathematical development, Primary survey report No. 3.* 1982, HMSO, Price £6.60

4.33   In the report on the third primary mathematics survey[1] one of the clusters described was entitled Area and perimeter. As can be seen from the primary items described here, the facilities for the same or similar questions were some 15 per cent to 20 per cent lower at the younger age level. The greatest and smallest differences occurred in R9, where for the perimeter question the primary and secondary facilities were quite close, but, in the part asking for the area, the primary facility fell by nearly 20 per cent giving a difference between the two age levels of 25 per cent. Some of the factors influencing performance and inducing errors were found to be the same; as at the secondary level, the facility of items was reduced if the terms 'area' and 'perimeter' were used and also as more complex shapes were given. There was also confusion between the terms 'area' and perimeter', with more pupils giving the correct perimeter when asked for the area than the converse error of giving the area when asked for the perimeter. A similar confusion occurred in the secondary practical topic on Length used in the 1978 and 1979 surveys. When asked what was the perimeter of a rectangle, nearly 8 per cent of the pupils answered 'length × breadth' with over 20 per cent not answering. The subsequent question asked pupils to describe how they would find the perimeter and, on this, 18 per cent of the pupils described a method of finding the area.

4.34 The general picture emerging from this collection of items is that around 85 per cent of the pupils were successful when considering area as covering a shape with a simple, basic unit and that over 70 per cent correctly answered similarly basic items testing knowledge of the terms area and perimeter. Facilities were lower when an unfamiliar unit was given, such as a half-centimetre square, expecially if no grid was provided and some amount of computation was required. Also, R3 and R6 suggested that as long as a grid was provided, a less regular shape had more effect in lowering the facility than a more difficult unit of area. Considerable, but varying, confusion between the terms 'area' and 'perimeter' was still present at the 15 year old level. Around 10 per cent of the pupils gave the perimeter when asked for the area with far fewer making the converse error when the computation was simple. However, when presented with higher numbers, nearly 20 per cent of the pupils opted to calculate the area (the more difficult calculation) instead of the perimeter. Conversely, the tendency to give the perimeter when asked for the area also varied, being lowest when a grid was provided (as in R11) and greatest when the question was set in a more practical context (R13). The last two items showed that there were many pupils who were confused about the relative lengths of a side and a diagonal of a square and of slanting lines. As well as the problems caused to pupils in questions on measurement and distance, this misunderstanding has implications in many areas of geometry, such as identifying the longest side of a triangle or even the hypotenuse of a right-angled triangle.

**Geometry**

*Rotation, reflection and symmetry*

4.35 In this cluster, a series of closely related items on reflection was used in an attempt to clarify the features which affect pupils' performance on this topic. In addition, another group of items on rotation is also discussed here as these two transformations are often confused by pupils.

P1

Draw the reflection of this shape in the mirror.

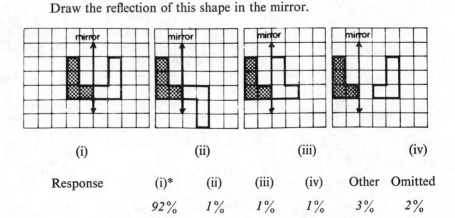

| | (i) | (ii) | (iii) | (iv) | | |

| Response | (i)* | (ii) | (iii) | (iv) | Other | Omitted |
|----------|------|------|-------|------|-------|---------|
| | *92%* | *1%* | *1%* | *1%* | *3%* | *2%* |

P2

Draw the reflection of this shape in the mirror.

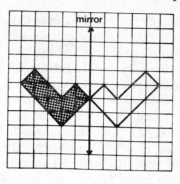

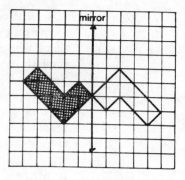

(i)                              (ii)

| Response | (i)* | (ii) | Other | Omitted |
|---|---|---|---|---|
| | 85% | 1% | 10% | 4% |

---

P3

Draw the reflection of this shape in the mirror.

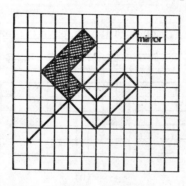

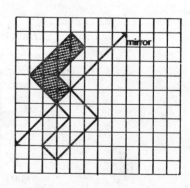

(i)                              (ii)

| Response | (i)* | (ii) | Other | Omitted |
|---|---|---|---|---|
| | 84% | 5% | 8% | 3% |

P4

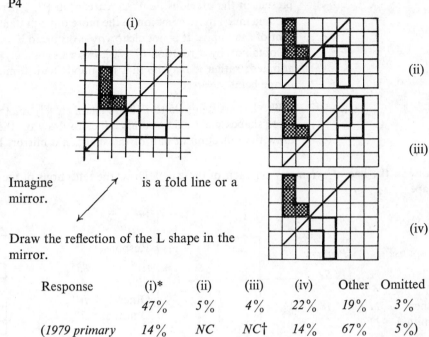

(i)

(ii)

(iii)

Imagine    is a fold line or a
mirror.

Draw the reflection of the L shape in the
mirror.

(iv)

| Response | (i)* | (ii) | (iii) | (iv) | Other | Omitted |
|---|---|---|---|---|---|---|
| | 47% | 5% | 4% | 22% | 19% | 3% |
| (1979 primary | 14% | NC | NC† | 14% | 67% | 5%) |

† *28% of 11 year olds in the 1979 survey placed the image in this orientation but at varying distances from the mirror.*

4.36   In Items P1 to P4 pupils were asked to draw the reflection of the same shape in a mirror, each time on a grid, but with the angle between the mirror and the grid and the angle between the shape and the mirror being varied in each item.

4.37   In the easiest of these, the mirror line was vertical and the edges of the L-shape coincided with the lines of the grid. Most pupils, 92 per cent, were successful on this item and there was no error that was particularly frequent.

4.38   In P2, the mirror line was still vertical but the shape was at 45° to the mirror and the grid. This proved only slightly more difficult than P1, with 85 per cent of the pupils answering it correctly. In P3, the mirror line was at 45° to the grid but the relationship between the shape and the mirror was kept constant so that the shape was also at an angle of 45° to the grid. This also proved slightly more difficult than P1, obtaining virtually the same facility as P2. Thus, changing the position of the shape with respect to the grid and the mirror line, or changing the angle of the mirror line and the shape but keeping them in the same orientation relative to each other was associated with a similar but small lowering of the success rate. In P4, however, while the shape was in the same position as in P1 relative to the grid, the mirror was placed at 45° to the grid so that the shape was at an angle of 45° to the mirror. This combination of a diagonal mirror and the shape at 45° to the mirror resulted in the considerably lower facility of 47 per cent. A common error in P4 was to reverse the image, in effect to rotate the shape through 180°. This error was present in the previous items (5 per cent in P3, 1 per cent in P1 and P2) but it became much more common in the more difficult item P4, being made by 22 per cent of the pupils. It is not clear why it occurred here but, even though it could be obtained by a rotation of 180°, it seems unlikely that this was the strategy adopted; rather it may be that the pupils had in mind some idea of a mirror image being reversed.

4.39   The six items P5 to P10 are again closely related through using the same three shapes and asking pupils either to draw on them a line of symmetry or draw the reflection of half of the shape in a mirror. In P5 and P6, 72 per cent

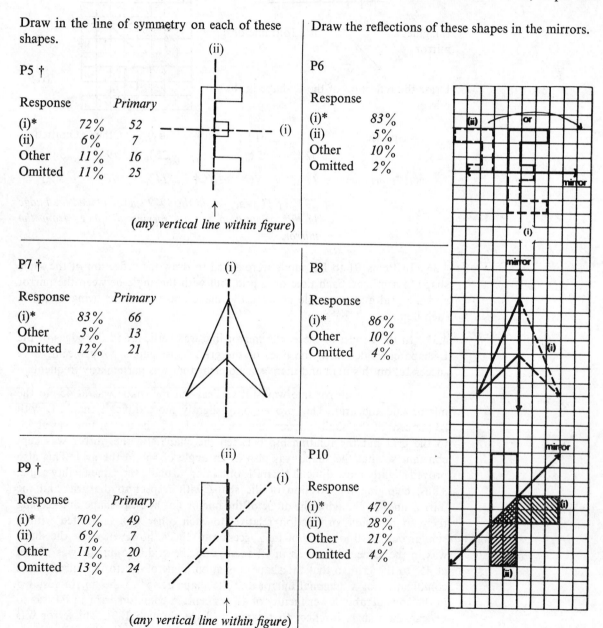

Draw in the line of symmetry on each of these shapes.

P5 †

| Response | | Primary |
|---|---|---|
| (i)* | 72% | 52 |
| (ii) | 6% | 7 |
| Other | 11% | 16 |
| Omitted | 11% | 25 |

(ii)

(i)

*(any vertical line within figure)*

Draw the reflections of these shapes in the mirrors.

P6

| Response | |
|---|---|
| (i)* | 83% |
| (ii) | 5% |
| Other | 10% |
| Omitted | 2% |

P7 †

(i)

| Response | | Primary |
|---|---|---|
| (i)* | 83% | 66 |
| Other | 5% | 13 |
| Omitted | 12% | 21 |

P8

| Response | |
|---|---|
| (i)* | 86% |
| Other | 10% |
| Omitted | 4% |

P9 †

(ii)

(i)

| Response | | Primary |
|---|---|---|
| (i)* | 70% | 49 |
| (ii) | 6% | 7 |
| Other | 11% | 20 |
| Omitted | 13% | 24 |

*(any vertical line within figure)*

P10

| Response | |
|---|---|
| (i)* | 47% |
| (ii) | 28% |
| Other | 21% |
| Omitted | 4% |

were able to draw the correct line of symmetry on a capital E while 83 per cent correctly drew the reflection of the top half of a capital E in the mirror. Similarly, in P7 and P8, a higher proportion of pupils drew the correct reflection than drew the correct line of symmetry, though with a smaller difference, 3 per cent rather than 11 per cent. The position was reversed with items P9 and P10; while a similar proportion of pupils, 70 per cent, drew the correct line of symmetry on the L-shape as drew the correct line on the capital E, considerably fewer, 47 per cent, drew the correct reflection. This was partly due to the high incidence of one particular error, that of continuing the lines straight across the mirror line to form a rectangle rather than an L-shape. This answer was given by 28 per cent of the pupils. Comparing items P10 and P4, which both have a mirror at 45° to the grid, it can be seen that the facilities of the two items are the same despite P4 containing a more complicated shape than P10.

4.40  In Item P11, pupils were asked to draw the reflection of a rather more complicated shape but this time without a grid. At first sight the high facility of 91 per cent may seem surprising in relation to the previous items. However, drawings by eye were accepted as correct provided they resembled the given figure, so that the absence of a grid acted as an advantage in the sense that a careless counting error could have caused some of the incorrect answers in the earlier items. Another contrast with one previous item, P10, is the different incidence of the error of continuing the shape straight across the mirror line. While present in P11, it was made by only 5 per cent of the pupils, with 2 per cent 'reversing' the mirror image. This type of error is possibly a result of the same mistaken conceptual understanding as the first two incorrect answers shown in P4. The high incidence of the particular error coded in P10 may well be explained by being the one most likely to be made by pupils with this mis-understanding, whereas in items P11 and P4 similar pupils make a greater variety of errors.

4.41  The same type of error occurred in one of the questions in the practical topic on Symmetry (see page 39). In this question pupils were presented with a line at an angle to a dotted line which they were told was a mirror line. 75 per cent drew an accurate, or near-accurate, reflection of the given line in the mirror, with 12 per cent making the error of continuing the straight line across the mirror. It is surprising that the success rate on the practical topic is nearly 20 per cent lower than the apparently more complicated item P11; the difference was accounted for by the presence of two errors, the one already mentioned and the other that of completing a V-shape.

4.42  It was also mentioned in Chapter 2 that in the 1979 practical survey the same question was used, but with the words 'line of symmetry' instead of 'mirror line'. As well as the success rate being some 25 per cent lower, the incidence of the error of continuing the line straight across was substantially greater at 32 per cent.

4.43  The remainder of this cluster is made up of two sets of items on rotation. One set gave a straight line on a grid in different positions and asked pupils to rotate the line through 90° about a given point. The other set gave pairs of lines of the equivalent rotations and asked pupils to mark on the grid the centre of rotation.

P11   Draw the reflection of this shape in the mirror.

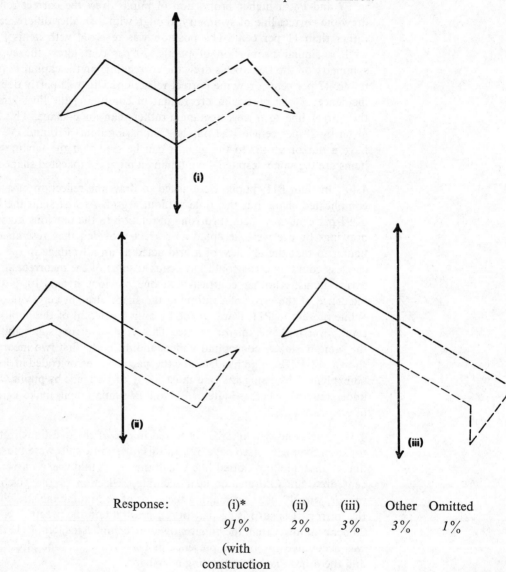

| Response: | (i)* | (ii) | (iii) | Other | Omitted |
|---|---|---|---|---|---|
| | *91%* | *2%* | *3%* | *3%* | *1%* |

(with
construction
lines: *17%*)

4.44   Looking at the items on page 99, it can be seen that there was a steep decline in the facilities of both sets of items as the rotation became more complex. P12, 13 and 14 were answered correctly by over half of the pupils, but the pairs of items P15 and 16, P17 and 18 and P19 and 20 were answered correctly by around 20 per cent of the pupils. Two general comments may be made about these last six items, firstly that the proportion either drawing the correct line or placing the centre of rotation is very similar and secondly that the proportion of pupils omitting the items, while increasing slightly through the set, remains

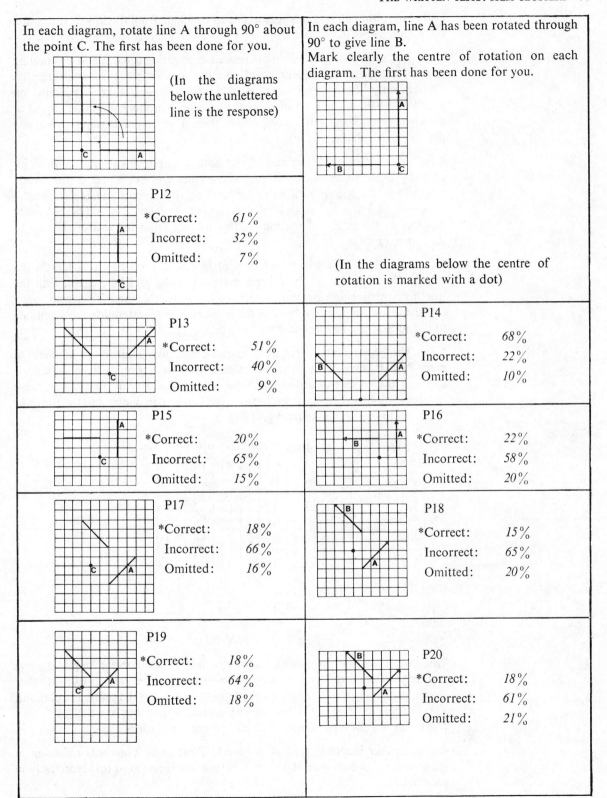

In each diagram, rotate line A through 90° about the point C. The first has been done for you.

(In the diagrams below the unlettered line is the response)

In each diagram, line A has been rotated through 90° to give line B.
Mark clearly the centre of rotation on each diagram. The first has been done for you.

(In the diagrams below the centre of rotation is marked with a dot)

P12

*Correct:    61%
Incorrect:   32%
Omitted:      7%

P13

*Correct:    51%
Incorrect:   40%
Omitted:      9%

P14

*Correct:    68%
Incorrect:   22%
Omitted:     10%

P15

*Correct:    20%
Incorrect:   65%
Omitted:     15%

P16

*Correct:    22%
Incorrect:   58%
Omitted:     20%

P17

*Correct:    18%
Incorrect:   66%
Omitted:     16%

P18

*Correct:    15%
Incorrect:   65%
Omitted:     20%

P19

*Correct:    18%
Incorrect:   64%
Omitted:     18%

P20

*Correct:    18%
Incorrect:   61%
Omitted:     21%

fairly low, although it seems reasonable to conclude from the low facilities that the requirements of at least the later items are unfamiliar to many pupils.

4.45 It is clear that a lot of care is needed in counting squares and positioning lines as well as an understanding of rotation to answer these items correctly. Consequently, the large proportion of incorrect answers that is indicated on page 99 is likely to be a result of counting errors, producing a large spread of different errors, as well as more conceptual misunderstanding producing possibly more characteristic errors.

4.46 On P12, nearly all of the 22 per cent of pupils answering the item incorrectly drew a line on the correct line on the grid but either of the wrong length or in the wrong position or both. Thus, they gave a line at right angles to the original line and placed it on the correct 'horizontal' grid line but made an error in the length of the line or the distance from the end of the line to the centre of rotation.

4.47 In P13, half of the 40 per cent of incorrect answers was a line in the correct direction and on the correct diagonal of the grid but, again, with the length or the position or both wrong. A few others, around 2 per cent, drew a V-shape, either from the base of the given line or by extending the given line to C and drawing the second arm from there.

4.48 The proportions of pupils attempting but giving incorrect answers to items P15, P17 and P19 were very similar. In each case, around 30 per cent drew a line in the correct direction as shown by line (a) in each item. Thus, these pupils gave a line at right angles to the given line but, in contrast to the previous items, no longer on the correct grid line.

P15          P17          P19

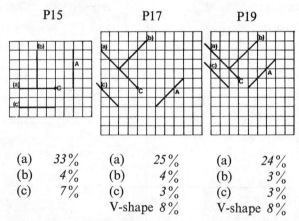

|     |        |     |        |     |        |
|-----|--------|-----|--------|-----|--------|
| (a) | 33%    | (a) | 25%    | (a) | 24%    |
| (b) | 4%     | (b) | 4%     | (b) | 3%     |
| (c) | 7%     | (c) | 3%     | (c) | 3%     |
|     |        | V-shape | 8% | V-shape | 8% |

4.49 Of these, the proportion drawing a line of the correct length starting two units away from C was 8 per cent in P15, and 6 per cent in P17 (in other words, preserving the distance of the end of the line from the centre of rotation). The proportion drawing a line of the correct length but starting at C was 7 per cent in P15, 5 per cent in P17 and 10 per cent in P19.

4.50 Another incorrect type of answer to these same items was reflection in a line either parallel to or at 45° to the given line (line (b) or (c) respectively in each item).

4.51 In items P17 and P19 another common incorrect answer, given by 8 per cent of the pupils, was a V-shape, that is a correct rotation through 90° but about the end of the given line rather than about C. Thus, in all the rotation items discussed here, a considerable proportion of the pupils giving an incorrect answer did give a line at right angles to the original line. In Items P12 and P13, many also drew such a line along the correct line of the grid, but made an error in its length or its exact position. In Items P15, P17 and P19, even though the facilities are all rather low at around 20 per cent, a further 30 per cent showed sufficient understanding of the concept of rotation to draw a line at right-angles to the original line but could not cope with the length and location of the end points of the line in relation to the centre of rotation.

4.52 In considering wrong answers to these items, it should be noted that the pupils were not provided with particularly large grids and, therefore, they may have been inhibited from making certain errors by the constraints of the grids.

4.53 Not surprisingly, there was a multiplicity of incorrect answers to the items asking for the centre of rotation, but some of the more common errors are shown in the diagrams below.

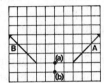 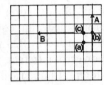 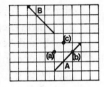 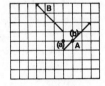

| (a) | 5% | (a) | 15% | (a) | 19% | (a) | 18% |
|-----|-----|-----|-----|-----|-----|-----|-----|
| (b) | 8% | (b) | 19% | (b) | 16% | (b) | 17% |
|     |    | (c) | 5%  | (c) | 4%  |     |     |

4.54 In this section, items on reflection and rotation have been reported on. In the first group of items on reflection, over 85 per cent drew the correct reflected shape provided there was not more than one complicating factor, (such as a diagonal mirror, object at an angle to the grid etc), but a combination of a diagonal mirror and the object at an angle to the grid produced a sharp decline in the success rate. In some of the reflection items there was a variable, but on occasions strong, tendency for pupils to adopt the incorrect strategy of continuing a line oblique to the mirror straight across the mirror line. The last group of items on rotation revealed a small proportion of pupils who were confused between reflection and rotation.

*Angles on a straight line and in a triangle*

4.55 The group of items discussed here was used to investigate the effect that different numbers, the use of letters for unknown angles and embedding figures in more complex figures had on the facility of items about angles on a straight line and in a triangle.

4.56 All the items in this cluster required knowledge of the angle sum of a triangle or of the angles on a straight line as well as the ability to manipulate either numbers or letters to obtain the required angle. Various features of the items were changed to discover whether certain conditions made the application of the knowledge or the manipulation required more difficult. In the first two items, the same two numbers are given and the third is asked for, in a triangle in P21, and on a straight line in P22. In both cases, the facility of the item was 75 per cent, with slightly more pupils not attempting the triangle item. P23 and P24 are two different variations on P21: in P23 the same triangle has been embedded in a larger figure and in P24 the numbers have been changed to make the computation more difficult. In both cases, the facility was lower than in P21, with embedding lowering the facility to 69 per cent, and the different numbers to 67 per cent. There was a small proportion of pupils in both items giving the total of the two given angles (this was not coded in P21) while in P24 the answer 53 was presumably a computational error in the subtraction, and 70° was probably obtained by pupils actually measuring the unknown angle.

4.57   Items P25 and P26 used a similar figure to P22, but set the problem in a more algebraic context. Although all that was needed to answer P25 correctly was the knowledge that angles on a straight line added up to 180°, it was clear from its lower facility (69 per cent) compared with P22 (75 per cent) that the algebraic form of the question had prevented some pupils who knew the geometric fact from answering correctly. The large number of 'other' responses which had been recorded in P25 were re-analysed to check whether there were any other common errors. In fact, the 21 per cent of pupils with 'Other' responses nearly all gave different numerical answers. Apart from 45°, given by 1 per cent, each different response, ranging from 3 to 760, was given by only one or two pupils. A few pupils appear to have measured the distances between the ends of the lines, and a few others to have measured the angles incorrectly, but it is not evident by what other processes most of this extensive variety of answers were obtained.

---

P21†

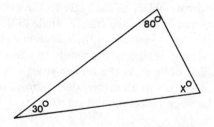

What is the value of x?

| Response | *70 | *70° | Other | Omitted |
|----------|-----|------|-------|---------|
| | 5% | 70% | 16% | 9% |

P22

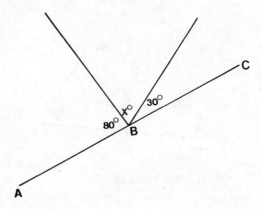

ABC is a straight line. What is the value of x?

.........................

| Response | *70 | *70° | Other | Omitted |
|----------|-----|------|-------|---------|
|          | 7%  | 68%  | 17%   | 8%      |

P23

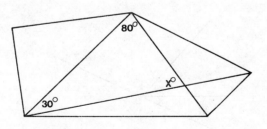

What is the value of x?

.........................

| Response | *70 | *70° | 110 | Other | Omitted |
|----------|-----|------|-----|-------|---------|
|          | 7%  | 63%  | 2%  | 23%   | 5%      |

P24

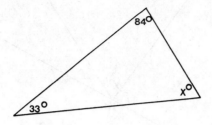

What is the value of x?

........................

| Response | *63 | 53 | 117 | 70 | Other | Omitted |
|----------|-----|-----|-----|-----|-------|---------|
| | 67% | 2% | 4% | 4% | 17% | 6% |

P25   ABC is a straight line.

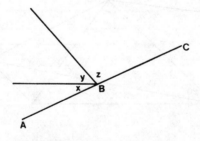

What do angles x, y and z add up to?

........................°

| Response | *180 | 90 | 360 | Other | Omitted |
|----------|------|-----|-----|-------|---------|
| | 69% | 2% | 1% | 21% | 7% |

P26    HFC is a straight line.

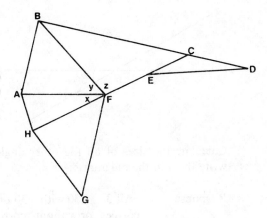

What do angles x, y and z add up to?

...................°

| Response | *180 | 90 | 360 | Other | Omitted |
|---|---|---|---|---|---|
| | *64%* | *2%* | *1%* | *24%* | *9%* |

4.58   In P26, the same three angles have been embedded in a larger figure and again the facility was reduced slightly to 64 per cent. Thus, from items P23 and P26 it can be seen that pupils are slightly less successful in answering questions on either a triangle or a straight line which have been embedded in a larger figure than the identical questions set with a straightforward figure.

4.59   In item P27 the computation required is again straightforward. However, fewer pupils were successful on this item with two intersecting straight lines (therefore, with just two angles on a straight line) than were successful on item P22. The facility of P27 was 65 per cent, which is 10 per cent lower than for item P22, and may be explained by the necessity of calculating all three angles correctly to be successful. However, the number of calculations required in P27 is really no more than in P22 and, in addition, very few pupils got two out of the three angles correct, which would be expected if some pupils were making computational errors. The most frequent wrong response, given by 6 per cent of the pupils, was to give 150° in incorrect answers for the other two angles. This suggests that 150° was obtained through knowledge of vertically opposite angles, but then a computational or some other error was made (though the required calculation, 180 — 150, is no more difficult than that required in P22). All this, and the fact that more pupils omitted P27 than P22, seems to indicate that pupils are less familiar with, or are more easily confused by, questions using vertically opposite angles than those using angles on only one side of a straight line.

P27

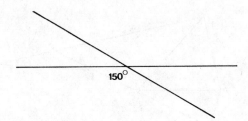

Calculate the sizes of all the other angles where these lines cross and write them in the diagram.

| Response | All 3 correct | 150 with or without other incorrect | 30 only correct | Other | Omitted |
|---|---|---|---|---|---|
| | 65% | 6% | 1% | 16% | 12% |

P28

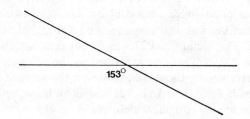

Calculate the sizes of all the other angles where these lines cross and write them in the diagram.

| Response | All 3 correct | 153+ incorrect | 27 only | 153 only | 150, 30 30 | Other | Omitted |
|---|---|---|---|---|---|---|---|
| | 52% | 6% | 5% | 1% | 5% | 19% | 12% |

P29†

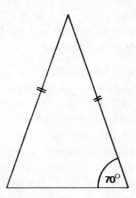

Calculate the other two interior angles of this isosceles triangle and write them in the diagram.

| Response | *70 & 40 | 70 only | Other | Omitted |
|---|---|---|---|---|
| | 59% | 11% | 16% | 14% |

P30

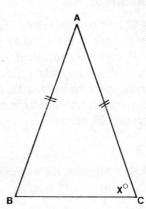

ABC is an isosceles triangle.

Give expressions in terms of x for the other two angles.

Angle A =     (i)
............

Angle B =     (ii)

(i)
............

| Response | *180—2x | 2x—180 | Expression with A, B | Numerical answer | Other | Omitted |
|---|---|---|---|---|---|---|
| | 20% | 1% | 2% | 20% | 30% | 27% |

(ii)

| Response | x* | | Expression with A, B | Numerical answer | Other | Omitted |
|---|---|---|---|---|---|---|
| | 41% | | 1% | 20% | 14% | 24% |

4.60   The effect of making computation more difficult can again be seen by comparing P27 and P28. In an otherwise identical question, P28 gave 153° instead of 150° and the facility obtained was 52 per cent, more than 10 per cent less than for P27.

4.61   Items P29 and P30 were concerned with an isosceles triangle, so that knowledge of the equal angle property of an isosceles triangle as well as the angle sum of a triangle was required. P29 is in numerical form, with one of the equal angles given. 70 per cent of the pupils gave the other 70° angle, but fewer, 59 per cent, gave the 40° angle as well. In P30 the same problem was set in algebraic form but, unlike P25 and P26, an algebraic expression is required in the answer, with the result that the facilities for both angles are considerably lower. While 70 per cent of pupils gave the other equal angle in numerical form in P29, nearly 30 per cent fewer gave the same angle when the answer was x°. Fewer pupils again, 20 per cent, gave the correct algebraic expression for the third angle. The facility of item P31, another algebraic item this time with a general triangle, was also 20 per cent. Comparing P21 and P31, it can be seen that 75 per cent of the pupils gave the correct third angle in a triangle when given the other two, but, when the three angles were given as letters, 20 per cent of the pupils gave the correct algebraic expression for one angle in terms of the other two.

4.62   From this collection of items it can be seen that about three-quarters of the pupils knew the angle sum of a triangle and of angles on a straight line and were able to calculate the third angle, given the other two. This success rate fell slightly when the computation was made more difficult or when the figure was embedded in a larger figure. The facilities for similar questions requiring algebraic expressions for the answers were considerably lower at around 20 per cent.

P31   Suppose the angles of the triangle were not known but were represented by a° and b°.

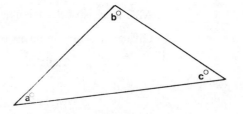

What is the value of c in terms of a and b?

........................

Response

| 180—a—b* | a+b+c* | 180—a+b | 45° | Other | Other | Omitted |
|---|---|---|---|---|---|---|
| 180—(a+b) | = 180 | 180—b+a | | numerical | | |
| 18% | 2% | 10% | 3% | 7% | 33% | 27% |

## Conclusion

4.63   In this chapter, the results for five different clusters of items drawn from three different areas of the mathematics curriculum have been described. The aim in all of these was, by using a collection of closely related items, to illustrate some of the factors influencing mathematics performance on particular topics and to highlight any sources of misunderstanding. The main variations in the items were in relation to their context, presentation and complexity. Some items were set either in a mathematical or a more everyday context; presentation was varied using different notation in the two Number clusters and by the presence or absence of a diagram in the Area and perimeter cluster; complexity was varied by using integral and non-integral dimensions in the Area and perimeter cluster, using different numbers for computations and, in the Rotation and reflection cluster, by changing the orientation of the mirror line.

4.64   These variations in different aspects of items had different influences on the levels of performance. Items about angles on a straight line and in a triangle were varied either by embedding a straightforward diagram in a more complex one, or making the computation less straightforward; both these variations were associated with small falls in performance levels. The item requiring pupils to draw a rectangle of equal area to a given rectangle was set with the answer involving either integral or non-integral dimensions; some 25 per cent fewer pupils were successful with the non-integral dimension. In the first four reflection items, an increase in complexity, by changing the angle of the mirror line or the orientation of the shape to the mirror, but not both, had little effect, but when these two were changed together there was a sharp decline in performance.

4.65   The different presentations used in some of the Number items often produced quite large changes in facility. The various ways of writing a square root produced different facilities as did the two alternative ways of asking for the cube of 4, in symbolic or verbal form. In the Division cluster, three of the ways of writing the same division had very similar success rates, but this fell when a ratio form was used and was lower again when a fraction was used. However, in the Area and perimeter cluster, the presence of a diagram seemed to be of no assistance when pupils were asked for the number of squares in a given rectangle. Also, items using the terms area and perimeter tended to obtain lower facilities than items asking directly for the number of units in a shape.

4.66   In the Area and perimeter cluster, two similar items in different contexts, mathematical and everyday, were used, for which the incidence of a particular error, as well as the success rate, changed. The item concerned the dimensions of a rectangle equal in area to a given rectangle; the success rate for this item set in an every day context was some 10 per cent lower than for the equivalent item set in a mathematical context and, also, the proportion of pupils adopting the incorrect strategy of preserving the perimeter more than doubled in the everyday item.

# 5 Attitudes

## The 1980 attitude questionnaire

5.1  An attitude questionnaire was administered to 15 year olds for the first time in the 1979 survey. The results of the initial administration led to some amendments being made this year. There were indications from a number of teachers of pupils in the sample that some pupils had taken over an hour to complete the questionnaire. Consequently, it was decided to omit one of the four sections used in 1979. The section dropped was the introductory set of open questions asking pupils about their favourite school subjects, their feelings towards mathematics and, in particular, those aspects of mathematics they found difficult and/or useful.

5.2  The remaining three sections formed the basis of the 1980 questionnaire. They were printed in a booklet in the order indicated below. Their composition was as follows:

(i)  A set of 36 statements expressing positive and negative opinions about mathematics. Pupils were asked to indicate the extent of their agreement or disagreement with each statement. Responses were coded and summed to form 3 scores measuring the degree to which they found mathematics to be useful, enjoyable, and difficult.

(ii)  A list of the names of 17 mathematical topics covering a wide range of the content of the mathematics curriculum. Pupils were asked to rate each in terms of usefulness and difficulty.

(iii)  A set of 17 items chosen from the written tests of concepts and skills. Pupils were asked to attempt each item and then to rate 'this type of problem' in terms of its difficulty, interest and usefulness.

[1]Azjen, I & Fishbein, M (1977). 'Attitude behaviour relations: a theoretical analysis and a review of empirical research'. *Psychological bulletin* 84, 394–400.

5.3  The first section was concerned with attitudes to mathematics as a subject discipline in the school curriculum; the second and third sections examined pupils' feelings towards particular topics within mathematics. There were two reasons for appraising attitudes to both general and specific aspects of mathematics. As mathematics covers a varying range of content for different individuals – apart from a core of topics, such as computation and measures – it seems advisable to investigate pupils' disposition towards topics, as well as the affective meaning the term 'mathematics' has for them. The second reason is that several researchers have recently suggested[1] that low correlations between attitudes and behaviour may be due to the lack of specificity in the measurement of these variables. This implies that there could be a closer association between attainment in specific mathematical topics and pupils' attitude towards them than is usually found between more general aspects of performance and attitude.

## Attitude to mathematics: questionnaire section I

5.4  The set of 36 statements formed the first section of the questionnaire. Pupils in the sample were asked to place a tick in one of the boxes adjacent to each statement; each box indicated a different degree of agreement with the statement from 'strongly agree' to 'strongly disagree'. A separate box was provided for those pupils who were undecided about their feelings. In 1979 there were 34 statements in the corresponding section. A factor analysis of the responses to these statements was carried out in order to sort the statements into scales. Three scales were identified, measuring pupils' difficulty with and enjoyment of mathematics, and the extent to which they thought it to be useful. The difficulty scale had 14 statements, the enjoyment scale 9 statements, and there were 11 statements assigned to the utility scale. These scales were distinctive, but not independent statistically and some statements correlated highly on more than one of them. For the 1980 survey, 4 of the statements were dropped either because they correlated highly with all 3 scales or because they were not related to any of them. Six statements chosen from the primary attitude questionnaire were substituted in order to facilitate comparison between the attitudes of the younger pupils with the 15 year olds.

[1] The similarity in structure was investigated by finding root mean square coefficients. (See H. H. Harman *Modern Factor Analysis.* University of Chicago Press, 1967. The coefficients for the scales were: difficulty 0.04, enjoyment 0.08, utility 0.23.

[2] The figures shown are percentages of the sample of pupils who completed the attitude questionnaire and do not always total 100 because of rounding to whole numbers.

5.5  The relationship to the 3 scales of the 30 statements common to the 1979 and 1980 questionnaires was similar in 1980 to that in 1979.[1] The statements relating to the usefulness of mathematics were responded to more strongly than those on the enjoyment and difficulty scales. The proportion of responses in the extreme categories (strongly agree or disagree) were generally between 5 and 10 per cent. The proportion ticking the extreme ends of the 5-point scale were well above this figure in response to the following statements on the utility scale:[2]

|  |  | Strongly Agree (SA) % | Agree (A) % | Undecided (U) % | Disagree (D) % | Strongly Disagree (SD) % |
|---|---|---|---|---|---|---|
| 1. When I leave school, I won't think again about most of the maths I've done | Boys | 6 | 23 | 7 | 41 | 23 |
|  | Girls | 9 | 29 | 8 | 38 | 16 |
| 2. It's hard to find a good job unless you've passed your maths exam | Boys | 38 | 39 | 6 | 12 | 4 |
|  | Girls | 32 | 43 | 9 | 12 | 4 |
| 3. Knowing maths is helpful in understanding today's world | Boys | 24 | 51 | 11 | 12 | 2 |
|  | Girls | 22 | 51 | 9 | 15 | 2 |
| 4. You won't be able to get on in life without a good knowledge of maths | Boys | 19 | 43 | 6 | 24 | 8 |
|  | Girls | 16 | 40 | 7 | 30 | 6 |

5.6   77 per cent of boys and 75 per cent of girls thought that a mathematics qualification is needed to find a good job (statement 2). About the same number agreed that mathematics is helpful to understand today's world (statement 3). Fewer pupils, but still over half of them, thought that mathematics would be of some general use to them after school (statements 1 and 4).

5.7   The statements on the enjoyment scale suggested that around 60 per cent of the pupils, boys and girls, find mathematics interesting. Statements 5 and 6 are examples.

|  |  | SA % | A % | U % | D % | SD % |
|---|---|---|---|---|---|---|
| 5. The more you study maths, the more interesting it becomes | Boys | 13 | 48 | 9 | 24 | 5 |
|  | Girls | 13 | 44 | 10 | 27 | 5 |

5.8   More reservations about the enjoyment of mathematics were noted when a statement, such as No. 6, implied that all of mathematics was interesting:

|  |  | SA % | A % | U % | D % | SD % |
|---|---|---|---|---|---|---|
| 6. I find maths lessons interesting, whatever we are doing | Boys | 6 | 29 | 12 | 42 | 11 |
|  | Girls | 7 | 25 | 11 | 46 | 9 |

5.9   As in 1979, there are statistically significant differences in the response of boys and girls to certain statements in the Difficulty scale:

|  |  | SA % | A % | U % | D % | SD % |
|---|---|---|---|---|---|---|
| 7. When it comes to doing a problem in maths I get all the formulas mixed up | Boys | 4 | 29 | 11 | 47 | 9 |
|  | Girls | 5 | 42 | 13 | 37 | 3 |
| 8. When I do well on a maths test, I consider myself lucky | Boys | 6 | 25 | 4 | 44 | 20 |
|  | Girls | 11 | 40 | 5 | 34 | 9 |
| 9. I can do the work in class but I don't know how to apply it | Boys | 5 | 31 | 16 | 43 | 7 |
|  | Girls | 7 | 43 | 13 | 34 | 3 |

5.10   The differences in the response patterns of boys and girls are largest in relation to statements concerning the difficulty of mathematics, and they are smaller when the statements refer to interest in mathematics or its usefulness. These results suggest that girls as a group have less confidence than boys in their mathematical ability. Fewer girls than boys thought they knew how to apply mathematics learned in the classroom (statement 9). Overall, as many pupils disagreed with statement 9 as agreed with it.

**Differences between 11 and 15 year olds**

5.11 Six statements from the primary questionnaire, relating to difficulty and utility, were included for the first time in 1980 so that a direct comparison could be made between the responses of the two age groups. The younger pupils, however, were given a 3-point scale (agree, disagree, unsure) from which to select their response. Consequently, in the following examples of these statements, the percentages of 15 year olds responding in the strongly agree and strongly disagree categories have been combined with the agree and disagree percentages respectively.

| | | Age | Sex | Agree % | Unsure % | Disagree % |
|---|---|---|---|---|---|---|
| 10. | I don't need maths much outside of school | 15 | B | 27 | 6 | 68 |
| | | | G | 32 | 7 | 60 |
| | | 11 | B | 19 | 20 | 61 |
| | | | G | 16 | 22 | 62 |
| 11. | I'm surprised if I get a lot of maths right | 15 | B | 36 | 9 | 55 |
| | | | G | 51 | 7 | 42 |
| | | 11 | B | 51 | 19 | 30 |
| | | | G | 59 | 20 | 21 |
| 12. | I can use maths to solve some everyday problems | 15 | B | 79 | 7 | 14 |
| | | | G | 68 | 9 | 22 |
| | | 11 | B | 83 | 12 | 5 |
| | | | G | 77 | 16 | 7 |
| 13. | Maths is one of my better subjects | 15 | B | 46 | 10 | 44 |
| | | | G | 30 | 11 | 59 |
| | | 11 | B | 51 | 23 | 26 |
| | | | G | 40 | 27 | 33 |

5.12 The differences between boys and girls at 11 were generally in the same direction as at 15. More of the younger pupils than the 15 year olds were unsure about their feelings, but this may be due to the use of a 3-point scale in the questionnaire for the 11 year olds.

**Relationship between the attitude scale and performance measures**

5.13 Pearson correlation coefficients were computed between pupils' scaled scores for the written tests of concepts and skills and their scores on each of the difficulty, enjoyment and utility scales. The scores for these scales were based on the 30 statements common to the 1979 and 1980 attitude questionnaires. For the purpose of this analysis, the performance scores used were those for mathematics as a whole. The correlations are given in Table 5.1.

**Table 5.1** *Correlations between attitude scales and performance*

| Scale | Boys (n= 528) | Girls (n=516) |
|---|---|---|
| Difficulty | −0.45† | −0.36† |
| Enjoyment | 0.15† | 0.10* |
| Utility | 0.27† | 0.23† |

† $p < .001$
* $p < .05$

5.14    The written test papers consisted of questions from 3 sub-categories out of 13 (see Chapter 3) and correlations were also computed between attitude scores on the 3 scales and the performance scores on each sub-category. The numbers of pupils involved for each combination varied between 80 and 190.

5.15    Correlations of boys' scores with the difficulty scale tended to be highest for traditional sub-categories and lowest for some modern sub-categories. For example:

| number applications | – 0.56 | statistics | – 0.27 |
| descriptive geometry | – 0.48 | modern geometry | – 0.33 |
| mensuration | – 0.48 | modern algebra | – 0.35 |

5.16    For the girls, scores in number skills had the highest correlation with the difficulty scale (—0.53 compared with —0.43 for the boys) and number applications the lowest (—0.18). All the correlations were statistically significant beyond the p = .05 level and most of them beyond the p = .01 level.

5.17    The highest correlations of attitude with performance for each sex were obtained for sub-categories in which mean scores were relatively high for the sex concerned. For example, descriptive geometry, mensuration and rate and ratio (items in this sub-category were included in number applications this year) are among those in which boys' mean score is high relative to that of the girls. In the number skill sub-category, girls' mean scores were closer to those of the boys' than in all but two other sub-categories.

5.18    The correlations of the enjoyment scale with the total performance score were low both for boys and girls. For individual sub-categories, the highest correlations for this scale were with number skills for both boys (0.23) and girls (0.28) and graphical algebra (0.24) for boys only.

5.19    The correlation of boys' scores with the utility scale was highest for number applications (0.42). On this scale, girls' scores correlated most highly with number skills (0.29).

5.20    One possible factor in these correlations is that pupils' attitudes to mathematics as a whole may be conditioned largely by only those topic areas which they consider most important.

## Attitudes to mathematical topics: questionnaire section II

5.21    As in 1979, a list of 17 topic names was given for rating by the sample pupils. There were, however, differences in the list this year, as compared with 1979, in several respects. Some of the topic descriptions were altered in response to suggestions by some of the teachers of the pupils in the 1979 sample; other mainly traditional topics in number and geometry, were replaced to accommodate some more modern topics, including 'vectors', 'matrices', 'statistics' and 'reflections and rotations'. In 1979, pupils were asked to rate the listed topics in terms of usefulness and interest. However, since the overall results of the 1979 attitude survey showed that difficulty was a more powerful component of attitude then interest, the 1980 sample was asked to rate the topics in terms of usefulness and difficulty. Another difference between the two surveys was that in 1980 pupils were able to indicate whether they thought they had 'not done' a topic. Each of the rating scales (usefulness and difficulty) consisted of 3 categories: not useful or difficult, fairly useful/difficult and very useful/difficult.

5.22    Topics perceived as most useful by the pupils were percentages, everyday problems, calculating with decimals, finding perimeter and area, and calculations with fractions – all traditional topics. Those perceived as least useful were reflections and rotations, matrices, vectors, sets and Venn diagrams (all modern mathematics topics), and working out algebraic expressions. Between 25 and 40 per cent of the pupils claimed not to have done these latter topics, but, even taking this into account, they are still considered the least useful of the 17 topics listed in this section. There was little difference between boys and girls in their perception of the usefulness of topics.

5.23    Topics rated as most difficult were: working out algebraic expressions, using formulae, problems in trigonometry, calculations with fractions, finding volume, measuring and calculating angles. The easiest topics were thought to be: using graphs and charts, using negative numbers, matrices, sets, Venn diagrams and vectors. Girls thought 13 of the 17 topics to be more difficult than did the boys, although only 4 of these differences reached statistical significance (volume, angles, perimeter and area, sets and Venn diagrams).

5.24    The usefulness and difficulty ratings were scored as follows: 2 points for a 'very useful' or 'very difficult' rating, 1 point for a 'fairly useful' or 'fairly difficult' rating and 0 points for a 'not useful' or 'not difficult' rating. These scores were then plotted. The results are shown in Figure 5.1. The mean ratings on both scales have been included (as dotted lines) and can be seen to divide the 17 topics into 4 groups as follows:—

|  | Useful | Not useful |
|---|---|---|
| Difficult | Angles<br>Volume<br>Fractions<br>Perimeter and area<br>Percentages | Algebraic expressions<br>Formulae<br>Trigonometry |
| Not difficult | Everday problems<br>Decimals<br>Graphs | Reflection and rotation<br>Statistics<br>Vectors<br>Sets<br>Matrices<br>Negative numbers |

Thus, modern topics were rated as neither difficult nor useful, while the traditional topics appear in each of the other quadrants of Figure 5.1 and the corresponding table above.

5.25   The results given in this section relate to topic names and so represented pupils' responses to some general idea of the topic. Examples of specific items might receive different responses. The third section of the questionnaire investigated this possibility.

**Figure 5.1**   *Difficulty and usefulness ratings of 17 topics*

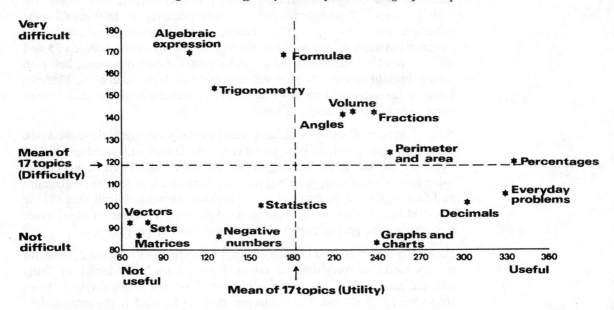

## Attitudes to concepts and skills items: questionnaire section III

5.26   In the final section of the questionnaire, 17 items from the written tests of concepts and skills were presented, one item per page. Pupils were asked to attempt the items and then rate them on three five point scales, in terms of their difficulty, interest and usefulness. The 17 items were made up by selecting one from each of the 17 topics in section II of the questionnaire; each item had a facility around the mean of the sub-category from which it came.

5.27   The relationship among the 3-ratings was investigated by computing correlation coefficients for the rankings of the items on the 3 scales. The correlations obtained are shown below. As in 1979, the association between utility and interest was the most marked.

|            | Difficulty | Utility | Interest |
|------------|------------|---------|----------|
| Difficulty | —          | 0.46    | 0.18     |
| Utility    |            | —       | 0.68     |

5.28   The ratings of usefulness and difficulty were ranked and compared with rankings of similar ratings of the corresponding topic names used in Section II

[1]Because of the different ways of presenting the items for rating in Section II and III, the topic names were rated on a 3-point scale and the maths items in Section III on a 5-point scale. The topic names were scored by giving 2 points for a 'very' useful/difficult response, 1 for a 'fairly' response and 0 for a 'not' response. The section III item ratings were scored using not sure as a neutral point.

of the questionnaire.[1] (There were no ratings of interest in Section II). There was little relationship between the rankings of topic names and corresponding items in relation to the difficulty scale (Rank correlation coefficient = 0.15). Thus, although pupils were instructed to respond to say how they felt "*about each kind of problem*", it appears likely that they responded largely to the specific content when judging the difficulty of an item. However, the rank correlation coefficient between ratings of the usefulness of named topics and the corresponding maths items was, in this instance, 0.95. Thus, modern mathematics topics such as vectors, matrices, sets, reflection and rotation were rated low in usefulness by the pupils, both generally and in relation to particular items but their perceived difficulty was different in the two modes. Both methods showed that boys, as a group, rate trigonometry, angles and formulae more highly than girls in terms of usefulness. Girls, overall, perceive everyday problems, decimals and fractions to be more useful than do the boys.

5.29   The facilities of the 17 items were compared with pupils' ratings of their difficulty in order to investigate the extent to which their difficulty was over or under-rated. The three items most over-rated in easiness were those on calculating the area of a square, an "everyday" cooking problem and one on reading a railway timetable. Two of these are illustrated below. The percentages of pupils responding in the very easy and easy categories were combined for this analysis.

---

To cook a joint of meat you should allow 15 minutes for each pound weight of meat and add an extra 20 minutes.

If the meat is to be cooked by 1 o'clock at what time should you start to cook a 4 lb joint? .......................

| | Boys % | Girls % | | Boys % | Girls % | | Boys % | Girls % |
|---|---|---|---|---|---|---|---|---|
| Very easy/ easy ratings | 81 | 79 | Facility | 52 | 55 | % ease minus % facility | 29 | 24 |

---

A square measures 12 centimetres right round its edge.

What is the area of the square? ....................... cm²

| | Boys % | Girls % | | Boys % | Girls % | | Boys % | Girls % |
|---|---|---|---|---|---|---|---|---|
| Very easy/ easy ratings | 76 | 65 | Facility | 33 | 28 | % ease minus % facility | 43 | 37 |

5.30   No item was under-rated in terms of easiness to such an extent as the above two examples were over-rated. The item most under-rated in terms of easiness was the one on percentages:

---

Some electrical stores will give discounts to certain people. One such person buys a record player priced at £50 in a store giving 5% discount, a television set priced at £350 at another store giving 7% discount, and an electric stove priced at £420 at a store giving 12% discount.

How much money will he have saved by getting discounts? ........................

  A.   £7.64
  B.   £9.89
  C.   £77.40
  D.   £95.00

---

| | Boys % | Girls % | | Boys % | Girls % | | Boys % | Girls % |
|---|---|---|---|---|---|---|---|---|
| Very easy/ easy ratings | 36 | 27 | Facility | 49 | 42 | % ease minus % facility | —13 | —15 |

---

5.31   The 'formula' and 'vectors' items' difficulties were also over-estimated by about the same amount. It was found that boys' estimates of item easiness, in relation to their success rate, were higher than those of the girls in 14 out of the 17 items.

## Conclusion

5.32   The questionnaire survey showed that about three-quarters of the pupils consider that mathematics is important to them in relation to a career and also in everyday life. As a group, girls' tend to believe, more than do boys, that mathematics is difficult; attitudes to individual problems suggest that boys tend to over-rate the ease of mathematical items, in comparison with girls.

5.33   Ratings of difficulty are found to be more highly correlated with performance than ratings of enjoyment or utility. However, if a topic is rated as useful, it is more likely to be thought interesting.

# 6 Problems, applications, investigations: a review of development

## Background

6.1  Since the surveys began in 1978, nearly all the items used in both the written and the practical assessments have tested pupils' mathematical skills and their understanding of mathematical concepts in various contexts. The assessment framework has also included categories of learning outcome relating to more general mathematical processes but, until recently, few such items have been developed.

[1]Kyles, I., Sumner, R., *Tests of attainment in mathematics in schools. Continuation of monitoring feasibility Study*. NFER. 1977.

6.2  The idea of developing ways of assessing a greater span of mathematical thinking, such as generalisation, proof and creativity, was first investigated in the monitoring feasibility studies known as TAMS[1]. These studies were in the nature of tentative probes and required further development before they could be accepted for use in the surveys.

[1]For list of participants see Appendix 4.1.

6.3  In 1979 a conference entitled "Problems, applications and investigations" initiated further development by the APU mathematics monitoring team. At this conference, teachers and researchers[1] presented their ideas on problem solving and investigating, and ways in which these activities could be assessed. Presentations were also made on models of problem solving and on methods and modes of assessment. The modes considered were written tests requiring short or longer responses, one-to-one interviews, mathematical investigations and group observation.

[1]See Appendix 4.2.

6.4  Following the conference, a number of ideas contributed by the participants were distilled into an initial framework of assessment categories and used to brief teachers' groups in Sheffield and Northern Ireland[1]. These groups had agreed to provide ideas for items and topics which might be included in the assessments.

6.5  The assessment categories were:

*Processing information*

Paying attention to relevant details, ignoring irrelevant details. Understanding sentences, tables, diagrams etc. Translating from one medium of communication to another e.g. from discourse to diagram, table or graph. Using notation.

*Formulating problems*

Given some information, focusing on some aspect of it and devising a problem or asking a question.

*Strategies and methods of solution*

Representing the problem using notation, graphs, diagrams etc. Reasoning: using mathematical, or other knowledge, to deduce a result.

*Generalising solutions*

Recognising patterns and relationships; continuing patterns. Generating patterns. Hypothesising generalisations.

*Proving*

Explaining and justifying results. Comprehending a logical argument. Constructing a logical argument. Detecting logical errors.

*Evaluating results*

Relating results to the original problem. Devising possibilities for the development of an investigation.

6.6   Given these categories, the teachers' groups provided a large number of ideas. Most of them, however, could be classified under two of the six headings, Strategies and methods of solution and Generalising solutions, but a few items involved interpreting graphs and tables under the heading Processing information.

## The development of written test items

6.7   The ideas provided by the teachers formed a basis for some written tests called 'problems and patterns' which were piloted in the 1980 surveys. Most of these related to the Generalisation and Strategies of solution categories and so reflected the balance of item types provided by the teachers' groups. The trialled items have since been amended in the light of the results of the pilot tests and two tests made up of the revised items have been included in the 1981 secondary survey.

6.8   Items in the Generalisation category, which were used in the pilot tests, took the form of a series of linked questions which examined pupils' appreciation of pattern, and asked them to explain the relationships involved. An example is shown in Figure 6.1 which illustrates the item given at the beginning of each test used to familiarise pupils with the format. Successive questions probe more deeply into pupils' awareness of the given pattern. The fourth and final question demands computational and other skills in addition to a deeper generalisation of the relationships between the numbers in each line of the pattern.

6.9   Another type of item explored pupils' performance in searching for all possible answers in a situation where several could be found; for example, the finding of the areas of different rectangles of a given perimeter.

6.10   Several members of the teachers' groups thought that items asking pupils to formulate problems and not actually to do them would be too unfamiliar to pupils. It was decided, however, to explore pupils' responses to being asked to provide problems rather than solutions in the 1980 pilot survey tests. One item provided pupils with some information about a packet of biscuits (Figure 6.2) and the pupils were then invited to make up any problems they liked using this information.

6.11   Figure 6.3 illustrates one approach taken to exploring pupils' strategies and methods of solving problems. In this item, some information and three related problems based on it are given. The answers to these problems and, in addition, descriptions of the methods used, are asked for.

**Figure 6.1**   *Trial item: recognising and continuing patterns.*

---

1.  Continue this adding pattern by writing
    the missing numbers in the blank spaces

$$0 + 1 = 1$$
$$1 + 2 = 3$$
$$2 + 3 = 5$$
$$3 + 4 = 7$$
$$4 + 5 = 9$$
$$5 + \quad =$$
$$\quad + 7 =$$
$$\quad + \quad =$$
$$\quad + \quad =$$

---

2a. Write here anything you notice about the answers to the additions in each line of the pattern.

 b. What do you notice about the other two numbers in each line?

---

3.  John says that this line belongs to the
    same pattern. Is he right? Explain.

$$14 + 16 = 30$$

---

4.  This line belongs to the pattern.
    Find the missing numbers and write
    them in the boxes.
    Show your working.

$$\boxed{\phantom{0}} + \boxed{\phantom{0}} = 57$$

**Figure 6.2**   *Trial item: formulating problems*

---

Tom bought 2 packets of Johnson's tea biscuits. He usually eats 3 biscuits a day, and he found that there were 12 biscuits in each packet.

Here is one question which could be answered from the information given:

a.  *How much does each biscuit cost?*

b.  To answer the question you need the cost of the packet (18p) and the number of biscuits in a packet (12).

c.   The cost of each biscuit is 18p ÷ 12.

Now think of some other questions which could be answered from the information given.

For each question say what you need to answer it and what you would do to answer it, but you do not need to work out the answer.

**Figure 6.3**   *Trial item: strategies of solution*

---

In a concert hall the seats are arranged in rows with the same number of seats in each row.

With 667 people in the hall, all the seats are taken and there are 19 people standing.

On another night, 554 people turn up when the last two rows are empty and 22 other seats are not used.

Show all your working.

a.   How many seats are there in the hall?
     How did you get that?                          .....................

b.   How many seats are there in each row?
     How did you get that?                          .....................

c.   How many rows of seats are there?
     How did you get that?                          .....................

## The development of practical test items

[1]APU *Mathematical development. Primary survey report No. 2.* HMSO, 1981.

6.12   The APU assessments are directed towards pupils across the whole range of ability. It was felt that lower ability pupils might be adversely affected by problems and patterns items which had an unusual format or were rather "wordy". As the practical mathematics mode was established to take account of such factors by introducing an oral test presentation in an interactive situation, it seemed highly appropriate to employ it also for assessing problem solving. In fact, some exploratory items were included in the practical surveys from the beginning, most of them in the primary practical tests. The first such item was included in the 1978 primary survey and was reported in the second primary survey report[1] described as "problem solving strategies".

6.13   In the 1980 secondary practical survey, a topic called "Tiles" was included which probed certain aspects of pupils' problem solving strategies, particularly those concerned with the abstraction of patterns and generalising. The results of this topic are described below as an illustration of the development of the problem solving assessments.

**Tiles:**

6.14   The purpose of this topic was to assess pupils' awareness of number patterns derived from certain configurations of 2cm square tiles and their ability to generalise the relationship between the patterns.

6.15   In this account of the results of the 'Tiles' topic, the items are printed as they appeared in the testers' scripts. In the scripts the questions put to pupils are printed in italic script and instructions to the testers in roman script. Some of the items include prompts which are given if certain responses are made by the pupils. In the tables of results, where relevant, correct responses are starred( * ). The first item in the topic presented the purpose of the exercise in very general terms and introduced the variables that were to be used.

---

1.   Remove 3 tiles from the bag.

*"This is an investigation about making shapes with these tiles and counting the distance around the outside for each shape. The tiles can only be joined edge to edge* (demonstrate with 2 tiles ) *or corner to corner* (demonstrate )."

Make this arrangement

*"If we say that each edge is one unit long, what is the distance round the outside of this arrangement?"* Trace the outline with your finger.

If wrong answer given, ask
*"Show me how you got that."*

---

†Responses:

|  | Boys | Girls | Total |
|---|---|---|---|
|  | % | % | % |
| No response | 0 | 1 | 0 |
| *10 | 79 | 80 | 80 |
| Other | 20 | 19 | 20 |

6.16   The 'other' responses were due to miscounting or misinterpreting the question: after the scripted prompt *"Show me how you got that"*, a further 14 per cent (12 per cent girls, 15 per cent boys) gave the correct answer and the remainder were shown what was required.

---

2a.   *"Now make an arrangement of the 3 tiles where the distance round the outside is less than 10."*

If unsuccessful, remind pupil of the two ways in which tiles may be joined together.

---

6.17   The second question served a number of purposes. It provided a check on whether pupils' had remembered the permissible configurations and also what was to be counted when they were asked for the smallest or largest perimeters.

6.18   It was also intended that this item should draw the pupils' attention to the idea of a relationship between the configuration of tiles and the distance around the outside.

Responses:

| | Boys % | Girls % | Total % |
|---|---|---|---|
| *□□□ | 66 | 65 | 65 |
| *⊏⊐ | 31 | 30 | 30 |
| Incorrect | 2 | 3 | 2 |
| No response | 0 | 2 | 1 |

6.19   In all, 95 per cent of the pupils produced one of the two configurations with a perimeter of 8 units without prompting. A further 3 per cent were successful after a reminder about the rules of the task and the remaining 2 per cent were shown how to get an answer.

6.20   The two-to-one ratio in favour of making the horizontal row of three tiles may be due to the ease with which the perimeter can be counted in that position or it may simply be produced by a strong tendency to push down the overhanging tile in the arrangement ⌐⌐ .

6.21   The next question was intended to set pupils thinking about a minimum perimeter for a given number of tiles.

---

2b.   *"See if it's possible to make an arrangement where the distance is smaller."* If pupil claims to have made a smaller distance or is uncertain, explain that 8 is the smallest.

---

6.22   Some pupils thought through this question without moving the tiles whereas others had to experiment before giving their replies.

Responses:

| | Boys % | Girls % | Total % |
|---|---|---|---|
| *"It's impossible": (tiles not moved) | 32 | 35 | 34 |
| *Decides its impossible after experimenting | 58 | 52 | 55 |
| Unclassified | 8 | 9 | 9 |
| No response | 2 | 2 | 2 |

6.23   At this point the table for results (see Figure 6.4) was presented to the pupils who were asked to fill in the first answer and also to explain it.

---

2c.   Present table for results.
*"Write your result in here. Why is that the smallest?"*

---

Responses:

|  | Boys % | Girls % | Total % |
|---|---|---|---|
| *Maximum number of sides hidden | 45 | 35 | 40 |
| *None of the tiles touch corner to corner | 5 | 2 | 3 |
| Can't make it any smaller | 21 | 20 | 21 |
| Unclassified | 19 | 25 | 22 |
| No response | 10 | 17 | 14 |

6.24   The first response was a completely satisfactory explanation and demonstrated those pupils' awareness of the most important feature of a configuration which reduced its perimeter. The second type of explanation was sufficient to explain that the perimeter was not a maximum for a given number of tiles, but not that it was the smallest.

6.25   Pupils providing the third explanation simply stated they were unable to make it any smaller and this was not considered adequate.

6.26   Following this item about the minimum perimeter was one on the arrangement of tiles which would produce a maximum perimeter.

**Figure 6.4**   *Tiles topic: table given to pupils*

| NUMBER OF TILES | DISTANCE ROUND THE OUTSIDE | |
|---|---|---|
|  | SMALLEST DISTANCE | LARGEST DISTANCE |
| 3 |  |  |
| 4 |  |  |
| 5 |  |  |
| 6 |  |  |
| 7 |  |  |
| 8 |  |  |

3a. *"What is the largest distance round the outside you can get with 3 tiles? Write your answer in the table."*

If incorrect say
*"There is a larger value."*

6.27   89 per cent of the pupils gave the correct response. The question did not demand the use of the tiles to arrive at the answer but most of the pupils chose to do so.

| | Boys % | Girls % | Total % |
|---|---|---|---|
| *12 | 54 | 54 | 54 |
| *12 | 19 | 25 | 22 |
| *12; tiles not used | 17 | 8 | 13 |
| Incorrect, tiles not used | 1 | 1 | 1 |
| Unclassified | 6 | 7 | 7 |
| No response | 3 | 5 | 3 |

6.28   Pupils who did not obtain the largest perimeter were told that there was a larger one and, after this prompt, 7 per cent more found the correct value.

3b. *"Why is that the largest?"*

Responses:

| | | Boys % | Girls % | Total % |
|---|---|---|---|---|
| 1. | *All 4 sides of each tile are showing | 65 | 65 | 65 |
| 2. | *None of the edges is touching | 23 | 17 | 20 |
| 3. | Can't make it any larger | 3 | 5 | 4 |
| 4. | Unclassified | 7 | 9 | 8 |
| 5. | No response | 3 | 3 | 3 |

6.29   85 per cent of the pupils gave an adequate explanation (responses 1 and 2) for 12 being the largest perimeter which could be made with 3 tiles compared with the 40 per cent who did so for the smallest perimeter (Q 2c). The main reason for this difference is almost certainly that it is easier to see and explain how the maximum number of sides can be shown than the minimum number. A subsidiary reason for the difference is probably due to the pupils' experience of the question about the minimum. Four per cent of the pupils gave an "empirical" explanation rather than one based on reasoning compared to 21 per cent who had done this in response to Q 2c. This difference was probably due to the relative difficulty of both understanding and explaining why a minimum configuration must be so.

4.    Present 4th tile.
      *"Arrange these 4 tiles so that the distance round the outside is as small as possible. Write your answer in the table."*

      If incorrect, say
      *"There is a smaller value."*

6.30    The items so far had established the nature of the task and tested pupils' understanding of it. An additional tile was now provided in order to explore whether pupils could apply their experience to further problems of the same type. It also introduced a special feature of the pattern for the minimum perimeter which is dependent on obtaining the most compact arrangement of tiles on each occasion. A square configuration is the most compact for a square number of tiles, not a chain or parts of a chain as in response 2 below. As a result, the minimum perimeter for 4 tiles (a square number) is the same as that for 3 tiles.

Responses:

| | | | Boys % | Girls % | Total % |
|---|---|---|---|---|---|
| 1. | * | ⊞ | 75 | 65 | 70 |
| 2. | | ▭▭▭▭ | 20 | 30 | 25 |
| 3. | Unclassified | | 3 | 1 | 2 |
| 4. | No response | | 0 | 1 | 0 |
| 5. | Uncoded | | 2 | 3 | 3 |

6.31    Those who did not obtain the correct response were prompted to look further. As a result, an additional 19 per cent of boys and 28 per cent of girls, (24 per cent total) were successful. So, ultimately, nearly all of those who initially made the chain (response 2) were able to spot the more compact square arrangement.

5.    *"What is the largest distance round the outside you can get with 4 tiles?"*
      *"Write your answer in the table."*

      If incorrect, say
      *"There is a larger value".*
      — provided not used earlier.

Responses:

| | Boys % | Girls % | Total % |
|---|---|---|---|
| * | 58 | 50 | 54 |
| * | 1 | 5 | 3 |
| * | 8 | 13 | 10 |
| * | 5 | 1 | 3 |
| * | 4 | 4 | 4 |
| *Answer given without experimenting with tiles | 16 | 17 | 17 |
| Unclassified | 8 | 10 | 9 |
| No response | 0 | 0 | 0 |

6.32   Most arranged the 4 tiles into a configuration with a perimeter of 16, but 17 per cent gave the answer without using the tiles; this was slightly higher than for those who did so in response to the same question using 3 tiles.

6.33   The proportion who found the correct largest perimeter for 4 tiles (91 per cent) was about the same as for 3 tiles (89 per cent). After the prompt, a further 4 per cent gave the correct answer.

---

6a.   *"Is it possible to make an arrangement where the distance is 11?"*

If pupil claims to have done so say,
*"Show me how you got that."*

If pupil uncertain after making attempts, tell him/her it's impossible.

---

6.34   This question was intended to draw attention to another feature of the perimeters, – they can only be even. In fact, a maximum perimeter for a given number of tiles must be a multiple of 4. In the case of a minimum perimeter, each additional tile eliminates one unit of length of an existing configuration and adds 3 units or, in the case of a tile which completes a square, eliminates two units and adds two units.

Responses:

| | Boys % | Girls % | Total % |
|---|---|---|---|
| *Impossible (without experimenting) | 28 | 41 | 35 |
| *Impossible (after experimenting) | 55 | 42 | 48 |
| Claims to have made one | 13 | 10 | 11 |
| Unclassified | 5 | 4 | 4 |
| No response | 0 | 2 | 1 |

6.35   Those pupils who claimed to have made an arrangement with a perimeter of 11 units found their error when asked to count the units. Those who were uncertain whether it was possible or not were told it was impossible.

---

6b.   *"Can you give me a reason why it's impossible?"*

If no response, say
*"Are there any other numbers you cannot make?"*

---

Responses:

| | Boys % | Girls % | Total % |
|---|---|---|---|
| *Acceptable | 12 | 8 | 10 |
| *Even numbers only | 45 | 44 | 45 |
| Incomplete explanations | 11 | 15 | 13 |
| Unclassified incorrect | 18 | 20 | 19 |
| No response | 14 | 13 | 13 |

The most frequent explanation given was that only even numbers were possible.

---

7.   Present 4 more tiles (making 8 in all).
*"Now complete the lines in the table for 5, 6, 7 and 8 tiles. You may use the tiles if you wish."*

*"There is a smaller/larger value"*
may be used if not already used.

---

6.36   This item explored pupils' awareness and understanding of what had so far been established about the relationship between the configurations of tiles and their perimeters and also their performance in continuing the patterns.

6.37   Responses (all pupils responded).

| | Boys % | Girls % | Total % |
|---|---|---|---|
| All correct | 80 | 81 | 81 |
| Largest all correct, some errors in smallest | 14 | 10 | 12 |
| Errors in both largest and smallest | 2 | 5 | 3 |
| Unclassified | 4 | 4 | 4 |

6.38   Testers were instructed to use the scripted prompt *"There is a smaller/larger value"* only once, as its constant repetition in the case of pupils who were continually failing to make the maximum and, especially, the minimum perimeter was thought to be discouraging. However, its use in these restricted cases resulted in a further 4 per cent of pupils obtaining a completely correct table.

6.39   Pupils' use of the tiles in arriving at results was also recorded. Not surprisingly, this differed for the largest and smallest perimeters.

| Methods | Boys % | Girls % | Total % |
|---|---|---|---|
| Did not use tiles for largest, experiments for smallest | 34 | 26 | 30 |
| Used tiles for some of smallest only | 4 | 3 | 3 |
| Used tiles for some of largest and all of smallest | 24 | 28 | 26 |
| Used tiles for all results | 36 | 39 | 38 |
| Unclassified | 3 | 3 | 3 |

6.40   Nearly a third of the pupils were sufficiently confident in their understanding of the relationship between the number of tiles and the largest perimeter to be able to calculate the latter without using the tiles. This was almost double the percentage who had not needed the tiles to find the largest perimeter for 4 of them (question 5). Only 7 pupils out of the 221 who took this topic made errors in both smallest and largest perimeters; six of these used the tiles to find all the largest perimeters and one for some of them. Although the use of tiles to find the largest perimeters may be an indication of some lack of confidence of pupils in their findings, 107 out of the 179 who obtained all correct results found them in this way.

6.41   At this stage nearly 90 per cent of the pupils appeared to have a firm idea of how to obtain the configurations which had the largest and smallest perimeters. The next questions (8, 9a, 9b) explored pupils' knowledge of the relationships between perimeter and number of tiles. The relationship between largest perimeter and number of tiles was easier to see and so the question about it was posed directly:

---

8.   *"Can you give me a rule for finding the largest distance round the outside for any number of tiles?"*
     If no response, say

     *"If you had 20 tiles, what would be the largest distance around the outside you could get?"*

     If response 3 (see below), say
     *"That's what you do with the tiles – how do you work out what the actual distance will be?"*

---

Responses:

| | | Boys % | Girls % | Total % |
|---|---|---|---|---|
| 1. | *Times/multiply by 4 | 42 | 37 | 40 |
| 2. | Add 4 each time/Go up in 4's | 21 | 21 | 21 |
| 3. | Refers to how tiles arranged | 22 | 25 | 23 |
| 4. | Unclassified | 3 | 6 | 5 |
| 5. | No response | 11 | 8 | 9 |
| 6. | Question not put to pupils who made errors in largest distances in Question 7. | 1 | 3 | 2 |

6.42   Of the two scripted prompts, 22 per cent of the pupils were given the first, 16 per cent the second and 4 per cent had both. After these prompts the following were added to the total which is given in the third column; (percentages given are of the total who took this topic).

| | | Boys % | Girls % | Total after prompt % |
|---|---|---|---|---|
| 1. | Times/multiply by 4 | 15 | 19 | 57 |
| 2. | Add 4 each time, goes up in 4's | 6 | 4 | 26 |
| 4. | Correctly predicts total for 20 tiles, no general rule given | 10 | 10 | 10 |
| 5. | Unclassified | 5 | 8 | (*Not applicable*) |

6.43   These results showed that a satisfactory generalisation of the rule for finding the largest distances was given by 57 per cent of the pupils (40 per cent before prompting). About a quarter of those who took this topic gave a general rule which was inadequate and a further 10 per cent could say what the result was for a specific number of tiles, without deriving a general rule.

6.44   Those pupils who had obtained correct answers for all the smallest distances were now asked to predict that result for 9 tiles. The remaining pupils were already having difficulties and were, therefore, not questioned further.

---

9a.   If all results for smallest distances are correct, continue
   "*If you had 9 tiles, what would be the smallest distance round the outside you could get?*"

9b.   "*How did you get that answer?*"

---

Responses:

| Answer | Boys % | Girls % | Total % |
|---|---|---|---|
| *12 | 5 | 7 | 6 |
| 14 | 68 | 62 | 65 |
| 15 | 13 | 10 | 12 |
| Unclassified | 2 | 8 | 5 |
| No response | 1 | 1 | 1 |
| Question not put to pupils who made errors in smallest distance in question 7 | 11 | 12 | 11 |

| Method | | | |
|---|---|---|---|
| 1. Pictured a 3 x 3 arrangement | 5 | 6 | 5 |
| 2. Imagined extra tile on 8 tile arrangement | 13 | 12 | 12 |
| 3. One more tile means adding 3 units | 9 | 8 | 9 |
| 4. Continued the pattern: two successive configurations remain the same then the next two increase by 2 units | 48 | 40 | 44 |
| 5. Add on 2 units | 7 | 10 | 9 |
| 6. Unclassified | 5 | 10 | 8 |
| 7. Not recorded | 2 | 2 | 2 |
| 8. Question not put to pupils who made errors in smallest distances in question 7 | 11 | 12 | 11 |

6.45 The pattern for the smallest distances is a particularly difficult one. The correct smallest distance for a square number of tiles can only be found by arranging the tiles in a square configuration. If the 9th tile is added to the configuration for 8 tiles, so that a 3 x 3 square results, the additional tile does not change the perimeter for it eliminates two units of the existing arrangement and adds two itself. 12 pupils said they pictured a 3 x 3 arrangement and 11 of these obtained the correct answer to this question; (the other one obtained 15 units). Another 27 pupils said they had imagined an extra tile being added to the 8 tile arrangement. Most of these (20) had obtained 14 units as their answer to question 9a; five more obtained 15 units. It is not clear from the recorded responses what arrangement had been imagined or how the answer 14 had been derived from it. The answer 15 was probably derived in the same way as the 19 pupils who provided method 3, (14 of these 19 had given the answer 15) —that an additional tile adds an extra 3 units, but forgetting that one of the existing units of perimeter is hidden when the new tile is placed in position.

6.46   Methods 4 and 5 appear to be based on reasoning solely from the number pattern rather than attempting to generalise what happens when an additional tile is added. The most frequent response was method 4 which 44 per cent of the pupils gave. Pupils providing this explanation were making a hypothesis which was entirely reasonable on the evidence of the entries in the table to date. These pupils noted that the smallest distance had remained the same for 3 and 4 tiles, for 5 and 6 tiles and also for 7 and 8 tiles and had increased by 2 units for each successive pair. A hypothesis that this pattern continued for 9 and 10 tiles predicted that the smallest distances for these numbers of tiles would both be 14. 97 out of 100 pupils who gave this method had predicted the smallest distance for 9 tiles would be 14. Method 5 (add on 2 units) given by 19 pupils could be a similar but less complete explanation than method 4.

6.47   The next item asked pupils to check their predictions about the smallest distance for 9 tiles and then to consider further the pattern of smallest distances by using more tiles, in preparation for attempting a generalisation.

---

10a.   *"Here are some more tiles* (present 8 more). *Investigate what the smallest distance is for other numbers of tiles. See if you can find a pattern. Start by checking your prediction for 9 tiles."*

Tell pupil to write down any results underneath the table.

*"There is a smaller value"*
may be used if not already used.

---

Responses:

| | | Number of tiles | | | | | | | |
|---|---|---|---|---|---|---|---|---|---|
| | | 9 | 10 | 11 | 12 | 13 | 14 | 15 | 16 |
| Correct smallest value | % Boys | 24 | 83 | 60 | 62 | 62 | 62 | 63 | 36 |
| | % Girls | 21 | 77 | 58 | 63 | 63 | 59 | 64 | 35 |
| | % Total | 22 | 80 | 59 | 62 | 62 | 61 | 63 | 36 |

6.48   After the scripted prompt, a further 40 per cent of the pupils obtained the smallest distance for 9 tiles making a total of 62 per cent who had done so. This figure was maintained for 11 to 15 tiles inclusive. Some 20 per cent more than this managed the smallest distance for 10 tiles and about 25 per cent fewer managed this for 16 tiles.

6.49   The reason for the larger percentage getting the correct result for 10 tiles is that they managed to do so in spite of failing to get the right answer for 9 tiles. These pupils had made a rectangular configuration for 8 tiles: and then added to the two layer chain for the 9 and 10 tiles:

This procedure gains the correct result of 14 units for the 10 tile arrangement. The pupils who did this were not so successful with the remaining arrangements.

6.50  This feature of the responses is demonstrated by the numbers who made an incorrect arrangement for each of the set of tiles – no one did this for 10 tiles.

|  |  | Number of tiles | | | | | | | |
|---|---|---|---|---|---|---|---|---|---|
|  |  | 9 | 10 | 11 | 12 | 13 | 14 | 15 | 16 |
| Incorrect arrangement | % Boys | 16 | 0 | 17 | 15 | 14 | 15 | 15 | 28 |
|  | % Girls | 15 | 0 | 15 | 11 | 9 | 14 | 10 | 25 |
|  | % Total | 16 | 0 | 16 | 13 | 12 | 15 | 13 | 27 |

6.51  The prompt was rarely invoked for the 11 to 15 tile arrangements but for the 16 tiles, a square number, it raised the number of correct responses by a further 11 per cent to 47 per cent overall. It should also be noted that 36 per cent obtained the correct response to 16 tiles without prompting, whereas 22 per cent had done so to 9 tiles, so fewer pupils needed reminding when the next square number appeared.

6.52  The next question asked pupils to make further predictions about the smallest perimeters which could be obtained with arrangements of from 17 to 21 tiles and with 25 tiles.

6.54  About 35 per cent were able to obtain the correct results up to 20 tiles, but for 21 and 25 tiles this proportion fell to about 25 per cent. By this time, questions were not being put to about 60 per cent of the pupils who had been finding them too difficult.

6.53  The following table (Table 6.1) shows the correct results for the smallest perimeters of from 3 to 100 tiles. The main feaure of the results picked out by 13 per cent of the pupils was the pattern of increase in the numbers of tiles which produced the same minimum perimeter ie. 2 sets of tiles have a perimeter of 8, 2 at 10, 3 at 12, 3 at 14 and 4 at 16 and 18 and so on. Two pupils said that the smallest perimeters of successive square numbers of tiles differed by 4 units.

*Description of pattern*

|  | Boys | Girls | Total |
|---|---|---|---|
|  | % | % | % |
| Recognises 2 at 8, 2 at 10, 3 at 12, 3 at 14 etc. | 11 | 15 | 13 |
| Square numbers go up in 4s' | 1 | 1 | 1 |
| Mentions square numbers but vaguely | 6 | 5 | 5 |
| Unclassified | 13 | 10 | 11 |
| Questions not put | 69 | 67 | 68 |

**Table 6.1**  *The pattern for the smallest distance.*

The pattern for the smallest distance is as follows:

| Number of Tiles | Smallest Distance |
|---|---|
| 3,4 | 8 |
| 5, 6 | 10 |
| 7, 8, 9 | 12 |
| 10, 11, 12 | 14 |
| 13, 14, 15, 16 | 16 |
| 17, 18, 19, 20 | 18 |
| 21, 22, 23, 24, 25 | 20 |
| 26, 27, 28, 29, 30 | 22 |
| 31–36 incl. | 24 |
| 37–42 incl. | 26 |
| 43–49 incl. | 28 |
| 50–56 incl. | 30 |
| 57–64 incl. | 32 |
| 65–72 incl. | 34 |
| 73–81 incl. | 36 |
| 82–90 incl. | 38 |
| 91–100 incl. | 40 |

The value of the smallest distance increases after the number of tiles is a square number and after each number mid-way between consecutive squares.

---

11. If pupil made false prediction in 9a but has now realised the pattern is not so obvious, say

   *"Can you be sure that the pattern for the largest distance continues as you first thought?"*

---

6.55   The purpose of this question was to see whether falsifying a prediction relating to the smallest perimeters would undermine their confidence in the pattern for the largest perimeters. This question was put to 50 per cent of the pupils.

Responses:

|  | Boys % | Girls % | Total % |
|---|---|---|---|
| Asserts that pattern for largest is correct | 43 | 46 | 45 |
| Uncertain about correctness | 4 | 5 | 4 |
| Unclassified | 2 | 0 | 1 |
| No response | 0 | 0 | 0 |
| Question not put | 51 | 49 | 50 |

6.56   Testers' comments on this topic indicated that many pupils had enjoyed the test. One tester added that *"Pupils were not expected to remember past facts but actually to think and describe what they thought"*. Some noted that pupils frequently miscounted and there were also comments about difficulties with describing and explaining relationships. The most frequently expressed complaint by the testers was about the injunction to use the prompt *"There is a smaller/larger value"* once only; some thought that this prevented several pupils from getting beyond question 9.

6.57    The situation in this topic produced two different number patterns, one of which (for the largest perimeter) was relatively simpler to spot and to generalise than the other (that for the smallest perimeter). Over half the pupils were able to give a general rule for the simpler pattern. The rule for the smallest perimeter was exceptionally difficult but about 1 in 8 pupils gave a description of the pattern which showed that they recognised how it would continue.

6.58    There were no consistent differences between boys' and girls' responses to this topic.

**Other practical mathematics topics**

6.59    The 'Tiles' topic is an example of problem solving in a mathematical context. Another of this type used in the 1980 practical survey was the 'Dominoes' topic. The 1980 survey also included an example of problem solving in a more "everyday" or "real" context: 'Journey to France'. In this situation, pupils were provided with a map giving information about Channel routes and car mileages from London to Paris and tables showing the costs of petrol and the Channel crossing in relation to various factors affecting the amounts involved. The costs of a trip from London to Paris were to be calculated.

6.60    The practical assessments in the first three secondary surveys have consisted of 10 to 12 topics built around a theme, concept or a piece of apparatus. In the final two surveys of the initial series of five, there will be 4 or 5 topics concerned solely with problem solving, and the problem solving element of topics relating to specific mathematical concepts is being increased.

## Conclusion

6.61    This chapter has reviewed the background and development of the assessment of some more general mathematical activities and processes. The work has derived from theoretical and practical studies which have been carried out in mathematics education by researchers and teachers.

[1]Polya, G. *How to solve it*. Doubleday Anchor, 1957.

6.62    A number of models of problem solving or classifications of problem solving processes have received attention in recent years. The best known of these is that produced by George Polya in his first book *How to solve it*[1]. Polya distinguishes four phases in problem solving.

Understanding the problem.

What are the data? What are the conditions?
What are the unknowns?

Devising a plan.

Connecting the date to the unknowns.
Think how to use a related problem.

Carrying out the plan.

Check each step.
Can each step be proved?

Reviewing the solution.

Can the result be derived differently?
Can the result be used for some other problem?

6.63   Polya suggests that heuristics, or discovery procedures, can assist the solver at each phase of the process. Polya's heuristics are listed above under each of the four phases. In some cases they consist of questions which the solver should ask about the task as provided or about the situation as worked so far. There are also suggested procedures such as '*think of a related problem*' which could link a new problem to a more familiar one and lead to a possible fresh line of attack on the former.

6.64   A number of teachers and researchers are investigating schemes for teaching problem solving which are related to heuristics[1]. Another approach is to identify the activities engaged in by mathematicians in the course of conducting an investigation, which is the most general of the exploratory processes[2]. These activities include specifying or formulating the problem, seeking a solution, generalising it and then proving the generalisation. The results can then be related to the original problem or, more broadly, to existing mathematical structures.

6.65   The above two approaches are generally concerned with situations which have a purely mathematical setting involving number and/or spatial representation. An explicitly applied approach is taken by educationalists concerned with what has come to be known as "real" problem solving[1]. The term "real" could be taken as referring to practical "everyday" situations which could occur at some time to most pupils, but many teachers committed to this approach insist that problems should, in addition, have an immediacy for the individual solving the problem. A sense of involvement, however, is an important ingredient of any problem solving situation.

6.66   It is these three approaches which are embodied in the title of this chapter, 'problems, applications and investigations' which was also the title of the conference referred to in the introductory section which initiated current APU work in this area. These approaches have different starting points but have much in common and can be considered as providing different emphases in a very broad and significant area of mathematical learning. Current research in learning and teaching is extending the original formulations of these approaches and also providing new ideas for assessment.

6.67   The assessment of problem solving and investigating can be carried out at different levels. Using the 'Tiles' topic situation described earlier as an example, it could be presented in a relatively open form e.g. "*Investigate the perimeters*

[1]See for example, Leone Burton's paper, 'The teaching of mathematics to young children using a problem solving approach.' *Educational studies in mathematics II* (1980) 43–58.

[2]For a review, see A. W. Bell, 'The learning of process aspects of mathematics.' *Educational studies in mathematics*, 10 (1979) 361–381.

[1]Open University, *Mathematics across the curriculum*, Course PME 233.

*of different arrangements of tiles*". This would require the pupil to formulate the problem and decide what aspects of the situation to investigate. A less open form of presentation, but one which still provides options so far as method is concerned, would be "*Find the maximum and minimum perimeters of tiles which can be placed corner to corner or edge to edge*". The situation as described in the 'Tiles' topic earlier in this chapter was presented in a more structured, progressive form which included questions aimed to evoke a number of components of the generalisation process. Finally, each component of a process or mathematical activity could be presented as a separate item in an open or closed form. Thus, the formulation of problems could be presented separately from doing them. Another example is the continuation of number sequences:

Fill in the missing numbers          1, ......, 4, ......, 32, ......

or Continue this pattern            1, 3, 5, 7,

or How many ways can the sequence beginning 1, 2, 4 be continued?

6.68   The APU assessments so far have included the structured approach and items testing separate components of the problem solving process. The written test items have, of necessity, been the more highly structured types of presentation. The practical interview mode of assessment has used items which first familiarise pupils with a situation and then lead towards more open exploration of patterns or rules than in the written test versions. Consideration is now being given to the possibility of using the practical mode for presenting complete problem or investigatory situations, especially more open ones, either to individual pupils or to groups. It is hoped that these will enable individual and creative approaches to mathematics to be assessed.

6.69   The results of the initial problems and patterns written tests and of the practical tests problem situations used in the 1981 and 1982 surveys will be published in a retrospective report to be written after the series of five surveys has been completed in 1982.

# 7 The pattern of results: a review of three surveys

## The pattern of results

7.1 The pattern of performance in the 1980 survey was similar to that observed in the first two surveys in 1978 and 1979. This applies to the results of the individual items, to the sub-categories common to all these surveys, and also to the pattern of subcategory scores against those background variables which have been used on all occasions. This year, new written test items were used and about 100 of those used in the 1978 and 1979 surveys were not included this time. Those items not used were mainly from four sub-categories: Applications of number, Rate and ratio, Probability, and Statistics.

## Individual items

**Item clusters: error analysis**

7.2 In Chapter 4 of this report, the results of individual items have been discussed within groups or clusters of items of related content. The items in a cluster differ in their presentation of the content or on the particular aspects of the concepts or skills they contain. These differences can then be related to any differences in the proportions of pupils making each type of coded response to the items.

7.3 The results from several clusters have shown that the incidence of some characteristic errors can be as high as 45 per cent and are, therefore, a major feature of the responses to items, and as much a guide to pupils' understanding as the success rate. Another aspect of the analysis of errors is that the incidence of particular errors can vary in relation to certain characteristics of the presentation or complexity of the content. The Powers and roots cluster discussed in Chapter 4 is a good illustration of these points.

| Item | Responses | | | |
|---|---|---|---|---|
| | Correct % | Halving % | Omit % | Others % |
| What is the square root of 16? | 76 | 4 | 9 | |
| $\sqrt{16} = \ldots\ldots$ | 71 | 3 | 16 | |
| Ring the number nearest to $\sqrt{200}$ 14, 100, 45, 20, 72 | 50 | 25 | 4 | Divide by 10 16 |
| $16^{\frac{1}{2}} = \ldots\ldots$ | 14 | 30 | 20 | Adding the $\frac{1}{2}$ (16.5) 14 |

7.4   It can be seen that the incidence of halving, instead of working out the square root of 16, in the above items was 4 per cent in response to a verbal presentation but 30 per cent when a fractional index was used. When the square root sign was used in relation to 16, the halving response was evoked in 3 per cent of the pupils but was given by 25 per cent when the number was 200. The rate of omission also varied in accordance with the type of presentation; for example, the multiple choice format produced a lower omission rate, as it usually does. Also, other responses were made to specific features of an item: 16 per cent of the pupils appeared to think that $\sqrt{200}$ could be obtained by dividing 200 by 10; 14 per cent added the fractional index to obtain the value of $16^{\frac{1}{2}}$. Because the incidence of particular errors varies according to the complexity of an item and to the context in which it is set, the tendency of a pupil to make an error may not be noticed in the classroom unless a range of items is provided.

**Differences in performance between 11 years and 15 years**

7.5   The high incidence of using the index as a multiplying factor in finding the value of $16^{\frac{1}{2}}$ is also notable as an example of an error which, in certain contexts, tends to persist from primary through secondary education. Nearly 50 per cent of 11 year olds made this kind of response to an item involving a power. The extent to which secondary pupils do this in relation to a variety of items was discussed in the second secondary survey report. Over the course of the first three surveys, an increasing amount of information has been gathered about the differences in performance levels between 11 year olds and 15 year olds and the extent to which characteristic errors persist during pupils' secondary education. In the second primary report, it was suggested that those persistent errors which have so far been identified are made to items which involve closely related concepts, for example, area and perimeter, the symbolic representation of addition, multiplication and powers, decimal notation and place value.

7.6   Differences in success rates between 11 and 15 year olds can be gauged from 95 items used this year in the written tests of concepts and skills which have also appeared in one or more primary surveys—twice the number of items which overlapped the two age levels in the first two surveys. The 11 year olds mean success rate on these items was 42 per cent (range 2 per cent to 88 per cent) compared with the older pupils' mean of 66 per cent (range 25 per cent to 96 per cent). This mean difference of 24 per cent compares with the rougher estimate of 15 to 30 per cent given in the first report for most of the items which could then be compared. In the number sub-categories, the 15 year olds' success rates increase by less than 24 per cent in concepts of fractions and adding or subtracting with fractions, and more than the mean on items about percentages and prime numbers.

7.7   The success rates of primary and secondary pupils on the questions relating to the pie chart below illustrate the differences in the older pupils' gains relative to the primary pupils in fractions and percentages.

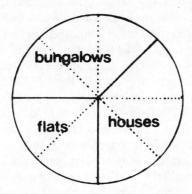

This pie chart shows the proportions of a class who live in different sorts of homes.

|  | *% Correct* | |
|---|---|---|
|  | *Primary* | *Secondary* |

What fraction of the class live in flats?

$\frac{1}{4}$ *or* $\frac{2}{8}$

...................      69      80

What percentage of the class live in flats?

*25*    % 

...................      23      61

What proportion of the class live in bungalows?

$\frac{3}{8}$

...................      30      47

7.8   The smallest difference between 11 and 15 year olds was obtained in response to the item $\frac{6}{10} + \frac{3}{10}$: 73 per cent of the younger pupils gave the correct response while 76 per cent of the 15 year olds did so.

7.9   The older pupils made large gains in items on descriptive geometry, reading scales and algebraic equations. Smaller differences between the two age groups were found on items involving sets and venn diagrams and the concept of area.

## The sub-categories

7.10   The previous section was concerned with the results for individual items. Each of the items used in the written tests of concepts and skills has been placed in one of the 15 content sub-categories of the framework (see Figure 1.1) and a mean scaled score computed for all the items in each sub-category. The method of doing this has been explained in Chapter 3. The score is derived from the success rate for each item and does not take into account the different kinds of errors made.

7.11   The items in each sub-category are intended to be representative of the range taught in the schools in England, Wales and Northern Ireland. Their representativeness has not been established by any detailed blueprint: the research team has judged the total balance and content from curriculum materials, text books and LEA guidelines. However, the development of the item collections has been supervised by the APU Mathematics Steering Group and comments have been received from many of the teachers whose schools have participated in the four surveys which have taken place at the time of writing. It was pointed out in the concluding chapter of the first secondary survey report that it would be possible to arrange for different mean scores by including a different mix of easy or hard items. However, the main purpose of classifying the items into the sub-categories is to obtain a more precise measure of performance in the bands of each background variable.

7.12   A number of consistent features are apparent over the three surveys so far in the pattern of sub-category scores against the background variables, and these are discussed in the following sections.

**Differences between regions**

7.13   There are five "regions", three in England (North, Midlands, South); the remaining two, Wales and Northern Ireland, are included as regions for the purpose of this analysis. The order of regional mean scores has been highly consistent over the three surveys within nearly all the sub-categories.

7.14   With a few exceptions, this order has been much the same in each of the sub-categories. Table 7.1 below gives the mean ranks over the three surveys of the sub-categories within each main content category, (1 representing the highest and 5 the lowest mean scores). Statistically, the differences between the regions have been most consistent between Wales and the South of England Generally, the differences between those two regions have been significant in all but one or two sub-categories. The differences between Wales and Northern Ireland have generally been statistically significant in about half the sub-categories. Other differences between regions have been smaller and the pattern of statistical significance not so clear cut.

[1]These differences can only be given approximately, firstly because there is some variation between surveys in their sizes, and, secondly, because of the way in which success rates in a sub-category are derived from the raw data.

7.15   The extent of the variation in the regional scores differs across sub-categories. The largest differences[1] appear in the modern sub-categories (Modern algebra, Modern geometry, Probability, and Statistics). For these sub-categories, the differences in mean success rates between Wales and the South of England are between 10 and 15 per cent. Since all the modern sub-categories are involved in this order of difference, it is likely that curriculum exposure plays a large part in producing these differences.

7.16   In other sub-categories, differences of up to 10 per cent in mean success rates have been obtained across the regions in Number applications and Graphical algebra. The range of variation has been smallest (around 5 per cent) in the sub-categories Number concepts, General algebra, Rate and ratio and Trigonometry.

**Table 7.1**  *Regional order of performance*

| | Region | | | | |
| Category | North | Midlands | South | Wales | Northern Ireland |
|---|---|---|---|---|---|
| Number | 4 | 3 | 1 | 5 | 2 |
| Measures | 3 | 4 | 1 | 5 | 2 |
| Algebra | 3.5 | 3.5 | 2 | 5 | 1 |
| Geometry | 2 | 3.5 | 1 | 5 | 3.5 |
| Probability and Statistics | 4 | 3 | 1 | 5 | 2 |

7.17  This picture differs from that for primary pupils in a number of respects. In Northern Ireland, 11 year olds had higher mean sub-category scores than those from other regions in almost all the sub-categories. Pupils from schools in the South of England had the highest mean scores (apart from Northern Ireland) at primary level in the newer areas of mathematics, but lower mean scores than pupils in Wales and Northern Ireland in the more traditional sub-categories. Pupils in Wales were second to Northern Ireland pupils in all the traditional areas of the curriculum at the younger age level.

7.18  It should be noted that the variations in pupils' mean scores within regions is greater than between regions, but the differences described above are consistent across three surveys. A variety of questions arise from the changing relative order between the regions during secondary schooling. For example, do the changes in relative performance relate to some topics within a sub-category, or are the changes general? Another question concerns the rate of relative change. Is it a steady change over the years of secondary education or is there a sharper change during a particular year or two? There are also issues which relate to differences in the curriculum at 11 and 15.

7.19  Some of these questions can be investigated further using existing data obtained from the surveys, but the relative rate of change could only be looked at by carrying out further surveys at other ages.

**Sex differences**

7.20  In all three surveys, the mean scores of the boys have been higher than those of girls in every sub-category, with only one exception: girls' mean scores were higher than boys' in Modern algebra in the 1979 survey. These differences have been statistically significant in up to eleven of the 15 sub-categories of content.

[1]The same caveat applies to the figures given here as was given to the size of the regional differences (See marginal note for paragraph 7.15).

7.21  The rank order of the sizes of the differences in boys' and girls' mean sub-category scores is fairly consistant across surveys; the results of the 1978 and 1980 surveys were particularly highly correlated. Full details of this ordering are recorded in Appendix 5; these show that boys' mean scores are largest relative to girls' in the Mensuration, Rate and ratio, Descriptive geometry, and Unit measures sub-categories. Over the three surveys, the boys' mean success rates in these areas have been about 8 per cent higher than girls'.[1] All these areas of mathematics are important in several secondary curriculum options such as the physical sciences, technical drawing and woodwork which are taken by more boys than girls.

7.22   Girls' mean scores are closest to boys' in Modern geometry, Number skills, Probability, Statistics, and Modern algebra. In these areas, girls' mean success rates have been, on average, about 1 to 2 per cent less than boys'. The most notable feature of this group of sub-categories is that nearly all the newer areas of the mathematics curriculum appear in them. There is no immediately apparent reason for this: it is not easy to envisage these areas as being of any crucial significance in the curriculum options taken by more girls than boys such as home economics, languages or art. The sub-categories in which girls' mean scores are closest to boys' are almost exactly the ones in which the 11 year old girls as a group do best relative to boys. In fact, 11 year old girls achieved higher mean scores than the boys in the sub-category Computation (whole numbers and decimals) in all three primary surveys so far conducted. The nearest parallel sub-category at age 15 is Number skills which includes fractions as well as whole number; there is some evidence from a study of a few items that 15 year old girls may have higher scores on the whole number items than on the fractions.

7.23   Some of the variations in the disparity between boys and girls found in the written test data have also been noted in a study by Sharma and Meigham of the results of GCE O–level examinations[1]. These researchers found that, on the whole, boys do achieve better O–level results than girls, but that such findings are misleading because mathematics experience is also obtained in other subjects such as science courses and technical drawing. Data on science courses taken by pupils in the 1980 APU mathematics survey shows that girls taking science courses tend to have higher mean scores than boys taking science courses. A number of factors could be responsible for this result; for example, it could be that girls only enter for science courses if their attainment in mathematics is high. In the USA, Fennema[2] has suggested that the *single most important influence on studying mathematics is studying mathematics*". She added that, where the amount studied is controlled, the statistically significant differences between boys' and girls' achievement in mathematics tend to disappear. However, the Cockcroft Committee in their report[3] point out that the evidence from the USA on sex differences in attainment needs to be confirmed in Britain.

7.24   Sharma and Meigham[1] found in their analyses of GCE data that "*the girls did better at some of the modern mathematics questions*'. It has already been noted that, in the APU survey data, 15 year old girls' mean scores in the 'modern' sub-categories are among those that are closest to the boys'. It is possible that girls find these topics of particular interest: the APU data on attitudes[2] found that "*whereas boys' performance was completely unrelated to whether or not they found a topic interesting, there was a significantly greater tendency for interest to be related to performance and perception of difficulty on the part of the girls*". However, this begs the question of why girls as a group should find modern mathematics particularly interesting, if indeed this is the case. Another possibility arises from the results of a survey of mathematics teaching in secondary schools in the Nottingham University Area Training Organisation[3] carried out in 1971. The report of this investigation states that "*contrary to the belief of some, the girls' schools have adopted more 'modern' texts than the boys. This could well be explained by the fact that many teachers are concerned*

[1]Shiam Sharma and Roland Meigham 'Schooling and sex roles. The case of GCE 'O' level mathematics.' *British journal of sociology of education* 1, 2. 1980.

[2]Fennema, E. 'Women and girls in mathematics' *Educational studies in mathematics*. 10, 389–401. 1979.

[3]*Mathematics counts*, HMSO, 1982.

[1]Shiam Sharma and Roland Meigham 'Schooling and sex roles. The case of GCE 'O' level mathematics. *British journal of sociology of education* 1, 2. 1980.

[2]*APU secondary mathematics survey report No. 2.* HMSO, paragraph 5.51. 1981.

[3]David Sturgess. *Mathematics teaching in secondary schools.* University of Nottingham School of Education.

*about the suitability of the modern syllabuses for boys who will follow engineering courses and trade apprenticeships on leaving school".* If this result holds true generally, it could explain some aspects of the relative performance of girls and boys in modern topics.

[1]Gina Baria Kolata, 'Math and sex: are girls born with less ability?' *Science* 210, December 1980.

7.25   Analyses carried out on the data from the 1978 and 1980 surveys have shown that the sex differences in performance are most marked in the upper attainment band. 62 per cent of the pupils in the top 10 per cent attainment band are boys and 38 per cent are girls. This type of finding has also been reported in the USA[1]. However, in the APU survey in the lowest 10 per cent band, the ratio of boys to girls is much smaller (48 per cent boys, 52 per cent girls). In fact, there are slightly more boys than girls among the very lowest scorers.

7.26   Further investigations are to be undertaken to study sex differences at the level of individual items, especially item clusters. These results should add a great deal of information on the variations in the differences in attainment of boys and girls.

7.27   The results to date suggest that many of the differences between boys and girls in mathematics attainment can be described as having two components: (i) profiles of relative strengths and weaknesses across the different areas of mathematics and (ii) the 'distance' between these profiles. Thus, in the Measures sub-categories at age 11, boys lead girls on average by about 6 per cent, but are behind the girls in Computation with whole numbers and decimals by about one or two per cent. There is a similar relative difference in the attainment of the two sexes in these areas of mathematics at age 15: in the Measures sub-categories, boys lead girls by around 8 per cent and they also lead by about 1 per cent in Number skills. At both ages, there is about 7 per cent relative difference between the boys' strongest and the girls' strongest areas, but between age 11 and age 15 the boys' profile of attainment moves up about 2 percentage points relative to the girls'. Whatever factors are causing the differences in the profiles of attainment are already operating by the time the pupils are in their primary schools.

**Other background variables**

7.28   The other background variables used in each survey have been:
Size of 15-plus age group (size of school in 1978).
Pupil/teacher ratio.
Location of school (metropolitan or non-metropolitan)
Percentage of pupils taking free school meals.

7.29   No pattern in performance with the size of the 15-plus age group has emerged over the three surveys.

[1]DES *Aspects of secondary education in England.* HMSO, 1979.

7.30   Location of school is an extremely broad variable which is misleading, particularly in areas such as Wales whose LEAs are all classified as non-metropolitan. Consequently, schools were asked this year to classify themselves in relation to the categories of catchment area used by HMI in their secondary survey.[1]

7.31   The overall results for the pupil/teacher ratio variable have been highly consistent across surveys and sub-categories within surveys. In all but one sub-category (the exception is Number concepts) schools in the middle band (15 to 17.5 pupils per teacher) have had the highest mean scores, followed by those with more than 17.5 pupils per teacher. The lowest mean scores have been obtained by those schools with the most favourable ratio of fewer than 15 pupils per teacher. Further investigation of the 1980 data in relation to the new catchment area variable has shown that the pattern for the overall sample occurred only in schools in prosperous suburban areas. The mean scores of pupils in inner city schools increased with increasing pupil/teacher ratio while for pupils in schools in rural and established manufacturing areas the opposite was the case: mean scores tended to decline with increasing pupil/teacher ratio. Pupil/teacher ratio is a school variable, not a pupil variable; it is a measure of the number of teaching staff in a school and gives no indication of the reason why staffing resources are high or low, or of the way in which the school deploys its staff. The results of both the primary and secondary surveys suggest that the tendency for mean scores to decrease with more favourable staffing ratios is strongest in inner city areas, and, in rural areas is non-existent (in the primary) or reversed (for secondary pupils). The association between pupil/teacher ratio and performance is, therefore, partly accounted for by affluence of catchment area, but more so for the secondary than for the primary pupils.

7.32   Information is being obtained on the size of group in which each sample pupil is taught and these data will be reported in a later publication.

7.33   Another consistent finding is that mean scores for pupils from schools in non-metropolitan LEAs are higher than those from metropolitan LEAs. Inner city pupils are generally from schools in metropolitan authorities; the more detailed HMI classification used this year showed that pupils from inner city areas had mean scores well below those from other types of area.

7.34   The percentage of pupils taking free school meals has been used to give some indication of the affluence of the school catchment area. For each survey, mean scores have increased considerably with a decrease in the percentage of pupils taking free school meals. There are now variations in policy between LEAs in relation to their provision of free school meals and, consequently, this variable will no longer be used after the 1980 survey.

7.35   The relationships reported above cannot reveal the reason for the association and their nature is not clear. A change in the value of one of these variables in schools will not necessarily produce a change in score which is in the direction of the association found in the surveys.

## Further investigations and future reports

7.36   Although there has been some fluctuation in the results obtained in the first three surveys, the most prominent feature of the data obtained on the separate occasions has been their consistency. Some patterns in the results have emerged and these have suggested some further investigations which are being undertaken and will be reported on subsequently.

7.37   However, it is not intended to publish a separate report on the fourth survey in this initial series of five. The next publication in this set will be a retrospective report which will evaluate the series of five surveys as a whole. The retrospective report will contain information relating to the results, over the five surveys, of each type of assessment instrument, and performance in each content area and learning outcome. The result of the survey pencil and paper tests on problem solving, which were employed for the first time in 1981, will be included.

7.38   There have been several references in this chapter to more detailed analyses of the data which are in progress or will be shortly undertaken. The results of these will be given in the retrospective report. The data from the complete series of five surveys should enable a valid judgement to be made about whether any trends in levels of performance have been present since 1978.

# Appendix 1. The survey sample and data collection

## A1.1 The sampling strategy

The sampling strategy adopted for this third survey of 15 year old pupils' performance in mathematics was very similar to that used for the first two. Full details are given in the report of the first survey. In deciding on the sampling strategy, a balance has been struck between the need for a sample large enough to allow useful inferences concerning the national population to be drawn and the need to avoid overburdening either schools or individual pupils.

A two-stage sampling procedure was used in which a stratified sample of schools was drawn first and, then, a sample of pupils was chosen from each selected school by reference to their dates of birth. The proportion of pupils selected from each sample school varied according to the size of the 15-plus age group in the school (the larger age group, the smaller the proportion of pupils sampled) since with this approach it is easier to predict the number of pupils who will be sampled at the second stage and more large schools are used, making it more likely that a representative sample of these schools will be obtained.

Since only a sample of the pupils in each school is tested, the two-stage sampling procedure demonstrates the Assessment of Performance Unit's declared intention of monitoring performance nationally and not concerning itself with the performance of individual pupils or schools.

## A1.2 Impact on schools and pupils

Schools had the option of not participating and of withdrawing individual pupils from the testing if it was thought likely to cause them undue distress. Although large scale withdrawals would have had serious consequences for both the representativeness and size of the achieved sample, it was felt that schools should be allowed this discretion. The extent to which it was exercised in this survey can be seen in Table A1.1. The effect of participation in the survey upon individual pupils was minimised by giving only a small number of the available items to each pupil and by keeping the testing sessions fairly short.

## A1.3 The survey sample

The target population was defined as all pupils born between 1 September 1964 and 31 August 1965, i.e. pupils whose sixteenth birthday fell between 1 September 1980 and 31 August 1981 inclusive[1]. Pupils in special schools or special units within schools were excluded.

It was intended to test approximately 10,000 pupils in England, and about 2,500 in each of Wales and Northern Ireland, i.e. about $1\frac{1}{2}$ per cent and 5 per cent of the age groups respectively. As described above, the proportion of pupils in the age group sampled in each school depended on the number of pupils in the 15 plus age group in the school, and the following proportions were used:

[1]These dates correspond to the school year in England and Wales. In Northern Ireland, however, the school year runs from 2 July to 1 July the following year. This means that in Northern Ireland, approximately five-sixths of the sample were 5th year pupils and the remainder 4th year pupils.

|  | Size of 15-plus age group | Proportion of age group tested |
|---|---|---|
|  | 4– 80 pupils[1] | 40% |
|  | 81–160 pupils | 20% |
|  | 161–240 pupils | 10% |
|  | over 240 pupils | 7% |

[1]Schools with fewer than four pupils in the relevant age group were excluded for administrative reasons.

In order to ensure that all regions of the country and all types and sizes of schools were represented, the population of schools in England and Wales was stratified in four ways: by type of school, size of the 15-plus age group, by region and by location as shown below:

| Type of school: | Comprehensive to age 16 |
|---|---|
|  | Comprehensive to age 18 |
|  | Other maintained |
|  | Independent |

| Size of 15-plus age group: | 4– 80 pupils[2] |
|---|---|
|  | 81–160 pupils |
|  | 161–240 pupils |
|  | over 240 pupils |

[2]Schools with fewer than four pupils in the relevant age group were excluded for administrative reasons.

| Region: | North |
|---|---|
|  | South |
|  | Midlands |
|  | Wales |

| Location: | In metropolitan counties |
|---|---|
|  | In non-metropolitan counties |

Details of the local education authorities in each region and their designation as metropolitan or non-metropolitan are given later in this appendix.

The schools in Northern Ireland were stratified for sampling by the size of 15-plus age group:

| Size of 15-plus age group: | 4– 80 pupils |
|---|---|
|  | 81–160 pupils |
|  | 161–240 pupils |
|  | over 240 pupils |

**Table A1.1**

(a)  *The sample of schools*

| | Number of schools | | | |
|---|---|---|---|---|
|  | England | Wales | N. Ireland | TOTAL |
| Invited to take part | 544 | 129 | 124 | 797 |
| Unable to take part | 43 | 6 | 14 | 63 |
| No reply | 12 | — | 7 | 19 |
| Initial agreement, but withdrew later | 3 | — | 1 | 4 |
| Test not received or returned unused | 5 | — | 5 | 10 |
| No pupils with selected birthdates | 2 | — | — | 2 |
| Tests received | 479 | 123 | 97 | 699 |

|  | England | Wales | N. Ireland | TOTAL |
|---|---|---|---|---|
| **Practical** |  |  |  |  |
| Schools taking part | 189 | 22 | 17 | 228 |
| **Attitudes** |  |  |  |  |
| Schools taking part | 123 | 32 | 30 | 185 |

(b)   *The sample of pupils*

|  | Number of pupils | | | |
|---|---|---|---|---|
|  | England | Wales | N. Ireland | TOTAL |
| Total sample | 9372 | 2348 | 2067 | 13787 |
| Absent | 312 | 82 | 41 | 435 |
| Withdrawn | 34 | 8 | 7 | 49 |
| Number completing tests | 9026 | 2258 | 2019 | 13303 |

Type of school:

Grammar controlled
Grammar other
Intermediate controlled
Intermediate other
Technical college

**A1.4   Written tests**

A sample of 797 schools was randomly selected within the stratification framework, and their headteachers contacted and asked if they, and their children, could take part in the survey. Table A1.1 gives details of the response rate achieved, with 699 schools providing data for the analyses described in this report.

The total sample of pupils for whom tests were sent to schools was 13,787 and, after absences and withdrawals, the tests from 13,303 pupils were returned to the NFER for marking (Table A1.1). Some of these were rejected subsequently for various reasons, e.g. faulty test booklets, answers illegible. In the event, test scores from 13,196 pupils were included in the analyses described in this report.

**A1.5   Practical tests**

A sub-sample was randomly selected for the practical testing from the schools and pupils taking the written tests. Thirty-one testers visited 228 schools and tested 1,140 pupils.

**A1.6   Attitude survey**

A different sub-sample of 1,073 pupils in 185 schools was randomly selected for the investigation of pupils' attitudes to mathematics.

**A1.7   Anonymity**

The APU is concerned about the anonymity of pupils taking part in the survey and it is agreed that pupils' names should not appear on any of the materials used in their assessments or be known outside the school. The procedure which has been adopted ensures the anonymity of the pupils tested while allowing checks to be made on the data.

A two-stage system is used in which teachers are asked to enter on specially designed Pupil Data forms the date of birth and sex of each of the pupils selected for the sample. These forms, made up of sets of direct-copying paper, are so designed that one copy is wider than the others to allow the name of the pupil to be entered alongside the date of birth. This copy is retained by the school. On receipt of the other copies of the form, containing only the date of birth and sex of each pupil, the NFER allocates a pupil reference number to each entry and one copy now containing the reference number as well as date of birth and sex is returned to the school so that the number can be entered on the school's copy containing the names of the pupils. Each test and questionnaire booklet subsequently sent to a school has one of the reference numbers allocated to the selected pupils in that school printed in advance on the front page. Names are not required and the test data are linked only to a reference number. The only link between the pupil's name and reference number is held by the school. Thus, the pupil's anonymity is not only preserved but also seen to be preserved.

It has also been agreed that schools and local education authorities will not be identified in any document or report produced by NFER for transmission to the DES, the Welsh Office, the DENI or for general publication.

**A1.8  Data collection**

The NFER followed its normal procedure of asking local education authorities for permission to contact schools under their control. This was given in all but one case in which the authority felt there were particular factors which argued for exclusion of the school. The schools were first contacted in July 1980, and were informed of the consultations which had already taken place with their LEAs and of the guaranteed anonymity of pupils, schools and LEAs. They were asked to agree to administer a test of about 50 minutes to some of the pupils in the age group.

Instructions for the testing were sent to schools about three weeks before the testing week and were followed by the tests themselves. Teachers were asked to make sure that each pupil completed the booklet allocated by a reference number to him or her. The way in which pupil reference numbers were allocated to the test booklets ensured that the 25 different written tests (see Chapter 3) were distributed at random throughout the sample of pupils. Testing was carried out in the week beginning 10 November 1980 and a further fortnight from the day of testing was allowed to test any pupil absent on that day.

Other information requested from the schools included the date of testing for each pupil or an indication of a pupil's absence or withdrawal, data concerning absenteeism and the numbers of pupils taking free school meals.

**Table A1.2**   *Counties in Regions in England and Wales*

| North | Midlands | South | Wales |
|---|---|---|---|
| Merseyside* | West Midlands* | Greater London* | Clwyd |
| Greater Manchester* | Hereford & Worcester | Bedfordshire | Dyfed |
| South Yorkshire* | Salop | Berkshire | Gwent |
| West Yorkshire* | Staffordshire | Buckinghamshire | Gwynedd |
| Tyne & Wear* | Warwickshire | East Sussex | Mid Glamorgan |
| Cleveland | Derbyshire | Essex | Powys |
| Cumbria | Leicestershire | Hampshire | South Glamorgan |
| Durham | Lincolnshire | Hertfordshire | West Glamorgan |
| Humberside | Northamptonshire | Isle of Wight | |
| Lancashire | Nottinghamshire | Kent | |
| North Yorkshire | Cambridgeshire | Oxfordshire | |
| Northumberland | Norfolk | Surrey | |
| Cheshire | Suffolk | West Sussex | |
| | | Isles of Scilly | |
| | | Avon | |
| | | Cornwall | |
| | | Devon | |
| | | Dorset | |
| | | Gloucestershire | |
| | | Somerset | |
| | | Wiltshire | |

*Metropolitan Counties

*Northern Ireland Education and Library Boards*

Belfast
North Eastern
Southern
South Eastern
Western

**Table A1.3**   *The obtained sample*

| Region & Location | Type | 4–80 Pupils | 4–80 Schools | 81–160 Pupils | 81–160 Schools | 161–240 Pupils | 161–240 Schools | 241+ Pupils | 241+ Schools |
|---|---|---|---|---|---|---|---|---|---|
| **NORTH** Non-Metropolitan | Comprehensive to 16 | 3 | 1 | 219 | 10 | 238 | 14 | 47 | 3 |
| | Comprehensive to 18 | 13 | 1 | 105 | 4 | 151 | 9 | 98 | 6 |
| | Grammar/sec. modern | 32 | 1 | 17 | 1 | 34 | 2 | 0 | 0 |
| | Independent | 68 | 4 | 13 | 1 | 0 | 0 | 0 | 0 |
| **NORTH** Metropolitan | Comprehensive to 16 | 28 | 1 | 213 | 10 | 151 | 9 | 35 | 2 |
| | Comprehensive to 18 | 0 | 0 | 157 | 8 | 295 | 17 | 348 | 18 |
| | Grammar/sec modern | 74 | 5 | 150 | 8 | 62 | 3 | 0 | 0 |
| | Independent | 49 | 4 | 138 | 6 | 0 | 0 | 0 | 0 |
| **MIDLANDS** Non-Metropolitan | Comprehensive to 16 | 27 | 1 | 274 | 13 | 139 | 8 | 28 | 2 |
| | Comprehensive to 18 | 0 | 0 | 149 | 6 | 344 | 18 | 189 | 10 |
| | Grammar/sec. modern | 85 | 4 | 145 | 8 | 22 | 1 | 0 | 0 |
| | Independent | 125 | 11 | 132 | 5 | 0 | 0 | 0 | 0 |
| **MIDLANDS** Metropolitan | Comprehensive to 16 | 0 | 0 | 84 | 4 | 47 | 3 | 17 | 1 |
| | Comprehensive to 18 | 0 | 0 | 75 | 4 | 80 | 4 | 75 | 5 |
| | Grammar/sec. modern | 11 | 1 | 30 | 1 | 0 | 0 | 0 | 0 |
| | Independent | 0 | 0 | 0 | 0 | 0 | 0 | 0 | 0 |
| **SOUTH** Non-Metropolitan | Comprehensive to 16 | 0 | 0 | 252 | 12 | 273 | 14 | 77 | 4 |
| | Comprehensive to 18 | 0 | 0 | 362 | 14 | 301 | 16 | 363 | 19 |
| | Grammar/sec. modern | 109 | 5 | 427 | 18 | 110 | 6 | 21 | 1 |
| | Independent | 551 | 36 | 117 | 5 | 0 | 0 | 0 | 0 |
| **SOUTH** Metropolitan | Comprehensive to 16 | 0 | 0 | 0 | 0 | 14 | 1 | 16 | 1 |
| | Comprehensive to 18 | 0 | 0 | 225 | 11 | 417 | 26 | 113 | 6 |
| | Grammar/sec. modern | 23 | 1 | 88 | 3 | 16 | 1 | 25 | 1 |
| | Independent | 224 | 12 | 17 | 1 | 22 | 1 | 0 | 0 |
| **WALES** | Comprehensive to 16 | 11 | 1 | 93 | 4 | 54 | 3 | 18 | 1 |
| | Comprehensive to 18 | 74 | 3 | 393 | 20 | 728 | 38 | 557 | 30 |
| | Grammar/sec. modern | 67 | 2 | 79 | 5 | 0 | 0 | 0 | 0 |
| | Independent | 166 | 15 | 0 | 0 | 0 | 0 | 0 | 0 |
| **NORTHERN IRELAND** | Grammar controlled | 46 | 2 | 102 | 4 | 32 | 1 | 0 | 0 |
| | Grammar other | 175 | 8 | 218 | 9 | 72 | 3 | 42 | 2 |
| | Intermediate controlled | 187 | 13 | 416 | 18 | 101 | 5 | 0 | 0 |
| | Intermediate other | 66 | 4 | 373 | 19 | 13 | 1 | 64 | 2 |
| | Technical college | 11 | 1 | 85 | 4 | 16 | 1 | 0 | 0 |

# Appendix 2.  Statistical significance

**A2.1   The meaning of statistical significance**

The purpose of drawing a random sample is to allow statistical inferences to be made about the defined population from which it was taken. Different samples drawn from the same population are subject to variations in their characteristics, so that their mean scores differ both among themselves and from the mean of the population. The larger the sample, the more precise its mean will be as an estimate of the population mean.

If it is desired to compare the performance of pupils in different defined sub-populations (for example, pupils aged 15 years from Northern schools and pupils aged 15 years from Southern schools), then separate samples would be drawn from each sub-population. What is required is to decide whether any difference between the sample means reflects a real difference between the sub-population means and the classical statistical significance test is designed to do this. The procedure is to calculate the probability that a difference in the sample means of the observed magnitude or higher would be found if the sub-populations in fact had the same means. If the probability of getting the obtained difference is low (e.g. 5 per cent or 1 in 20 chances) on the assumption that the sub-populations are the same, then the difference between the sample means is said to be statistically significant at that level of probability (i.e. at the 5 per cent level). Such a significance test may also be viewed as a device for providing evidence about the direction of the difference, so that a statistically 'significant' result is strong evidence that the difference between the sub-population means is in the same direction as that of the sample means. A 'non-significant' result simply fails to provide such evidence.

Thus, if a difference between two sample means is significant at the 5 per cent level, this only means that, if there was no difference between the sub-populations from which the samples were drawn, such a difference could be expected to arise by chance between no more than 1 pair of samples out of 20 (i.e. 5 per cent). It follows that if 20 independent differences between sample means are tested at the 5 per cent level it is to be expected that one of them will be "significant" *even if there is no real difference* between the sub-populations sampled. This proviso should be particularly noted in the context of the data from the written tests and background variables where a very large number of significance tests have been carried out.

Statistical significance does not provide an indication of the educational significance of a difference between the defined populations. Thus, a statistically non-significant large difference between sample means may be more worthy of note for further investigation than a statistically significant small difference between sample means; the former needs to be supported statistically, but the latter might be of little interest educationally even if it was a real difference. Throughout this report, therefore, references are made to statistically significant results which must then be judged in relation to their possible educational significance and implications, both of which are usually left to the reader.

**A2.2   The tests of significance used for this report**

Throughout the analyses for this report, statistical significance has been determined by computing the statistic $\bar{z}$ described in Chapter 9 of *Fundamental statistics in psychology and education* by J P Guilford and B Fruchter, fifth edition, published in 1973 by McGraw-Hill. The standard error terms given by Guilford and Fruchter have, however, been modified to make allowance for the inflation (the "design effect") arising from the use of a stratified cluster sample rather than a simple random sample. The estimated design effect on the variance of the sub-category scores is 1.7 for the 1980 data and this has also been used as an estimate of design effect for the practical and attitude data. A detailed discussion of cluster sampling and design effect is to be found in *Survey sampling* by Leslie Kish, published in 1965 by Wiley.

# Appendix 3. The development of the practical tests

| | Name | School |
|---|---|---|
| **A3.1 Practical testers in the 1980 survey** | Mr P D Bailey | Earls High School, Halesowen. |
| | Mr R Beattie | Bangor Girls' High School, Co. Down. |
| | Mr R Butcher | Menzies High School, West Bromwich. |
| | Mr G W Cobb | Lavington Comprehensive School, Nr. Devizes. |
| | Mr K Dyson | Gillingham School, Dorset. |
| | Mrs C Fenton-Coopland | Wingfield Comprehensive School, Rotherham. |
| | Mr A George | Ysgol Gyfun Llanhari, Pontyclun. |
| | Mr C Glover | The Castle School, Thornbury, Bristol. |
| | Mr D Gordon | Limavady Secondary School, Co. Londonderry. |
| | Mr D Gowing | Deighton High School, Huddersfield. |
| | Mr P G Hamill | St. Peter's Secondary School, Belfast. |
| | Mrs E Hampson | St. John Houghton School, Ilkeston, Derbyshire. |
| | Miss L Harper | The Neale-Wade School, March, Cambridgeshire. |
| | Mrs A Hugill | Sir Thomas Picton School, Haverfordwest. |
| | Mr D James | Penryn School, Cornwall. |
| | Mr E Jones | Rooks Heath High School, South Harrow. |
| | Mrs S M Jones | Wardle High School, Rochdale. |
| | Mr M Leonard | Education Dept., Walsall. |
| | Miss S. Marshall | Wyke Upper School, Bradford. |
| | Mr D J Morley | Hall Mead School, Upminster. |
| | Mr A R Mozley | St. George's High School, Blackpool. |
| | Mr P Nokes | St. Thomas More High School, Denton, Manchester. |
| | Mr R Perkins | Education Dept., Hounslow. |
| | Mr G Saltmarsh | Queen Elizabeth's School, Crediton, Devon. |
| | Miss C Savage | Holy Trinity School, Crawley. |
| | Mr V Schwarz | The Henry Meoles School, Moreton, Wirral. |
| | Mr A R Watson | Harton Comprehensive School, South Shields. |
| | Mr J E Watson | Education Dept. St. Helens. |
| | Mr D Wellman | Bexley Grammar School, Welling. |
| | Mr B Williams | Ysgol John Bright, Llandudno. |
| | Mr G Woodhouse | Shene School, London, S.W.14. |

**A3.2 Teachers assisting with development**

The following teachers tried out draft versions of topics in their own schools and we are grateful for the assistance they provided with the development work.

| Name | School |
|---|---|
| Mrs H J Boyce | Crayford School, Kent. |
| Mr A Horrocks | Gateacre Comprehensive School, Woolton, Liverpool. |
| Mr W McCullough | Park Parade Secondary School, Belfast. |
| Mr D J Maxwell | Tynemouth Teachers Centre, North Shields, Tyne and Wear. |
| Mr D B Steer | Riley Senior High School, Hull. |
| Mr B R Thomas | Montsaye School, Kettering. |

**A3.3  Schools assisting with development**

The following schools kindly provided facilities for interviewing pupils during the development of the topics for the 1980 survey.

> Cannon Palmer High School,
> Aldborough Road South,
> Seven Kings,
> Ilford,
> Essex.

> Claremont High School,
> Claremont Avenue,
> Kenton,
> Harrow,
> Middlesex.

> Streatham Hill and Clapham High School for Girls,
> Wavertree Road,
> London,
> S.W.2.

**A3.4  Videotapes of pupil interviews**

At the briefing of testers for the practical survey, videotapes of pupil interviews were shown.

We should like to thank the London Borough of Richmond-upon-Thames and the following schools in that Authority for providing facilities for videotaping interviews with their pupils.

> Orleans Park School,
> Richmond Road,
> Twickenham.

> Whitton School,
> Percy Road,
> Whitton.

# Appendix 4. Development of the assessment of problem solving

**A4.1 Participants in APU Conference (1979): Problems, applications, investigations.**

In addition to members of the APU Mathematics Steering Group and the Monitoring Team, the following participated:

| | |
|---|---|
| Ms Ruth Eagle | University of Keele, Department of Education |
| Dr Tom Gorman | NFER, Language Monitoring Team. |
| Mr Bruce Horton | Nottingham University Shell Centre for Mathematical Education |
| Prof. David Johnson | Centre for Science Education Chelsea College |
| Mr Eric Love | Wyndham School Egremont, Cumbria |
| Dr John Mason | Open University Walton Hall, Milton Keynes |
| Mr Graham Ruddock | Polytechnic of the South Bank Department of Professional Education Studies |
| Dr Christine Shiu | Nottingham University Shell Centre for Mathematical Education |

**A4.2 The teachers groups**

The following groups assisted the Monitoring Team with the development of items for the problems and patterns tests described in Chapter 6.

*Sheffield Group*

| | |
|---|---|
| Mr F Kurley—Convenor | Assistant Head, Rowlinson School |
| Mr D St John Jesson—Chairman | Lecturer in Mathematics Education, Arts Tower, Sheffield University |
| Mr D Allen | Deepcar St. John Primary School |
| Mr D Barratt | Headmaster, Gleadless Middle School |
| Mr J Booth | Deputy Head, Greenlands Middle School |
| Dr D A Bryers | Deputy Head, Wickersley School, Rotherham |
| Mr J Donald | Ashleigh School, Gleadless Road |
| Mr K Hides | Headmaster, Westways Middle School, Crookes |
| Mr D Kirkby | Sheffield City Polytechnic |
| Mr I Russell | Deputy Head, Herding's Primary School, Norten Avenue |
| Mrs S Sturgeon | Colley School |
| Miss P Thorpe | Rowlinson School |
| Mr D Wilson | Lecturer in Mathematical Education, Sheffield City Polytechnic |

*Belfast Group*

| | |
|---|---|
| Dr I Wells—Convenor | Senior Research Officer, NICER |
| Mr R McKinney—Chairman | Headmaster, Avoniel Primary School |
| Miss I Boland | Senior Inspector, DENI |
| Mrs V Boyle | Head of Mathematics, Dunmurry High School |
| Mrs M Deboys | Head of Remedial Department, Lisnasharragh Primary School |
| Mr D Falloon | Inspector, DENI |
| Dr B Greer | Lecturer, Department of Psychology, Queen's University, Belfast |
| Miss M Hillen | Headmistress, St Kevin's Girls' Primary School |
| Mr W McCullough | Deputy Headmaster, Park Parade Secondary School |
| Dr H Morrison | Mathematics Department, Belfast Royal Academy |
| Mr M Murray | Inspector, DENI |
| Mr L Patterson | Primary Seven, Finaghy Primary School |
| Mr S Smyth | Headmaster, St Joseph's Primary School, Antrim |

*Londonderry Group*

| | |
|---|---|
| Mr D Vaughan—Convenor | Western Education and Library Board |
| Dr I Wells—Secretary | Northern Ireland Council for Educational Research |
| Mrs R Allen | Newbuildings Primary School |
| Mrs M Doherty | Holy Child Primary School |
| Mr S Dunn | New University of Ulster |
| Mr D Gordon | Limavady Secondary School |
| Mr J McCourt | Waterside Boys' Primary School |
| Mr D McDermott | Carnhill High School |
| Mr M McDowell | Department of Education for Northern Ireland |
| Mr E McEleavy | St Columb's College |
| Mr P McLaughlin | Rosemount Primary School |
| Mr A Morgan | Carlisle Road Primary School |

# Appendix 5. Statistical appendix to chapter 7

**A5.1  Order of regions within each sub-category**

In Table A5.1 the mean scaled sub-category scores for Wales, Northern Ireland, and the regions of England are ranked within sub-category for each of the three surveys.

N   =   North of England

M   =   Midlands

S   =   South

W   =   Wales

NI  =   Northern Ireland

The sub-categories are listed by code letters as follows:—

F:          Number concepts
H:          Number skills
J:          Applications of number

R:          Unit measures
K:          Rate and ratio
Q:          Mensuration

M:          General algebra
U:          Traditional algebra
N:          Modern algebra
V:          Graphical algebra

P:          Descriptive geometry
B:          Modern geometry
S:          Trigonometry

W:          Probability
X:          Statistics

[1]Siegel, S. *Nonparametric statistics.* McGraw Hill, 1956.

Friedman 2-way ANOVAs were used[1] to test, within each sub-category, the null hypothesis that the rankings of the regions over the three surveys were equal i.e. came from the same population. The rankings were found to be significantly different at the $p = .025$ level for sub-categories N and V, at the $p = .05$ level for sub-categories F, U, B and S, and just beyond that level for sub-categories H, Q, M and P.

In the case of the four sub-categories which have appeared in their original form in two surveys only (those which are starred) the test was applied to the rankings for those two surveys only.

**Table A5.1** *Order of regions within sub-category for three surveys*

| Survey Sub-category | 1978 Region | | | | | 1979 Region | | | | | 1980 Region | | | | |
|---|---|---|---|---|---|---|---|---|---|---|---|---|---|---|---|
| | N | M | S | W | NI | N | M | S | W | NI | N | M | S | W | NI |
| F | 4 | 2 | 1 | 5 | 3 | 3 | 4 | 1 | 5 | 2 | 4 | 2 | 1 | 5 | 3 |
| H | 3 | 4 | 2 | 5 | 1 | 3 | 4 | 2 | 5 | 1 | 5 | 2 | 3 | 4 | 1 |
| J | 3 | 4 | 1 | 5 | 2 | 3 | 4 | 1 | 5 | 2 | 3 | 4 | 1 | 5 | 2* |
| R | 3 | 4 | 1 | 5 | 2 | 2 | 4 | 1 | 5 | 3 | 3 | 2 | 1 | 5 | 4 |
| K | 4 | 5 | 1 | 3 | 2 | 2 | 3 | 1 | 5 | 4 | 2.5 | 4.5 | 1 | 4.5 | 3.5* |
| Q | 4 | 3 | 2 | 5 | 1 | 3 | 2 | 1 | 5 | 4 | 4 | 2 | 1 | 5 | 3 |
| M | 3 | 4 | 2 | 5 | 1 | 4 | 5 | 2 | 3 | 1 | 4 | 3 | 1 | 5 | 2 |
| U | 3 | 4 | 2 | 5 | 1 | 3 | 5 | 2 | 4 | 1 | 4 | 3 | 1 | 5 | 2 |
| N | 4 | 3 | 2 | 5 | 1 | 4 | 3 | 2 | 5 | 1 | 4 | 3 | 2 | 5 | 1 |
| V | 4 | 3 | 1 | 5 | 2 | 4 | 3 | 1 | 5 | 2 | 4 | 3 | 1 | 5 | 2 |
| P | 3 | 4 | 1 | 5 | 2 | 2 | 3 | 1 | 4 | 5 | 3 | 2 | 1 | 5 | 4 |
| B | 4 | 3 | 1 | 5 | 2 | 4 | 3 | 1 | 5 | 2 | 3 | 2 | 1 | 5 | 4 |
| S | 3 | 5 | 1 | 4 | 2 | 2 | 4 | 1 | 5 | 3 | 2 | 3 | 1 | 5 | 4 |
| W | 4 | 2 | 1 | 5 | 3 | 3 | 4 | 1 | 5 | 2 | 4 | 3 | 1 | 5 | 2* |
| X | 3 | 4 | 1 | 5 | 2 | 4 | 2 | 1 | 5 | 3 | 4 | 3 | 1 | 5 | 2* |

| 3 survey total of ranks | | | | | 3 survey rank of total | | | | | |
|---|---|---|---|---|---|---|---|---|---|---|
| N | M | S | W | NI | N | M | S | W | NI | p |
| 11 | 8 | 3 | 15 | 8 | 4 | 2.5 | 1 | 5 | 2.5 | .05 |
| 11 | 10 | 7 | 14 | 3 | 4 | 3 | 2 | 5 | 1 | .075 |
| 9 | 12 | 3 | 15 | 6 | 3 | 4 | 1 | 5 | 2* | .10 |
| 8 | 10 | 3 | 15 | 9 | 2 | 4 | 1 | 5 | 3 | .05 |
| 8.5 | 12.5 | 3 | 12.5 | 9.5 | 2 | 4.5 | 1 | 4.5 | 3* | .40 |
| 11 | 7 | 4 | 15 | 8 | 4 | 2 | 1 | 5 | 3 | .075 |
| 11 | 12 | 5 | 13 | 4 | 3 | 4 | 2 | 5 | 1 | .075 |
| 10 | 12 | 5 | 14 | 4 | 3 | 4 | 2 | 5 | 1 | .05 |
| 12 | 9 | 6 | 15 | 3 | 4 | 3 | 2 | 5 | 1 | .025 |
| 12 | 9 | 3 | 15 | 6 | 4 | 3 | 1 | 5 | 2 | .025 |
| 8 | 9 | 3 | 14 | 11 | 2 | 3 | 1 | 5 | 4 | .075 |
| 11 | 8 | 3 | 15 | 8 | 4 | 2.5 | 1 | 5 | 2.5 | .05 |
| 7 | 12 | 3 | 14 | 9 | 2 | 4 | 1 | 5 | 3 | .05 |
| 11 | 9 | 3 | 15 | 7 | 4 | 3 | 1 | 5 | 2* | .20 |
| 11 | 9 | 3 | 15 | 7 | 4 | 3 | 1 | 5 | 2* | .20 |

*These sub-categories were incomplete in the 1980 survey and the ranks were averaged relative to the remaining sub-categories over the other two surveys.

A5.2 **Order of sex differences in sub-categories between surveys**

In the following analysis, the differences between boys' and girls' mean sub-category scaled scores have been ranked within survey. The ranks for the four incomplete sub-categories in the 1980 surveys have been averaged relative to the remaining sub-categories over the other two surveys.

**Table A5.2** *Rank order of differences in boys' and girls' scores for each sub-category in three surveys*

| Sub-category | Survey 1978 | Survey 1979 | Survey 1980 | Total of ranks | Rank of total |
|---|---|---|---|---|---|
| F | 7 | 9 | 5 | 21 | 6 |
| H | 10 | 12 | 11 | 33 | 12 |
| J | 12 | 4 | 8* | 24 | 8 |
| R | 6 | 1 | 4 | 11 | 4 |
| K | 3 | 2 | 3* | 8 | 2 |
| Q | 2 | 3 | 2 | 7 | 1 |
| M | 4 | 8 | 6 | 18 | 5 |
| U | 5 | 11 | 7 | 23 | 7 |
| N | 14 | 15 | 15 | 44 | 15 |
| V | 8 | 5 | 12 | 25 | 9 |
| P | 1 | 7 | 1 | 9 | 3 |
| B | 9 | 10 | 10 | 29 | 11 |
| S | 11 | 6 | 9 | 26 | 10 |
| W | 13 | 14 | 13* | 40 | 13 |
| X | 15 | 13 | 14* | 42 | 14 |

*These sub-categories were incomplete in the 1980 survey and have been averaged relative to the remaining sub-categories over the two surveys.

The Spearman rank correlation co-efficients between surveys are:—

| | |
|---|---|
| 1978–1979 | 0.64 |
| 1978–1980 | 0.90 |
| 1979–1980 | 0.72 |
| Mean | 0.75 |

The Kendall Co-efficient of Concordance[1] for this mean produces a $\chi^2$ of 35 (df = 14) which is significant beyond the p = .001 level.

The Spearman rank correlation co-efficients between surveys for the 11 sub-categories common to all three surveys.

| | |
|---|---|
| 1978–1979 | 0.45 |
| 1978–1980 | 0.85 |
| 1979–1980 | 0.56 |
| Mean | 0.62 |

The value of W for this mean produces a $\chi^2 = 22.4$ (df=10) which is significant beyond the p = .05 level.

[1] Seigel, S. op. cit.

**Table A5.3**   *Order of bands of pupil/teacher ratio variable (PTR)*

| Survey | 1978 PTR | | | 1979 PTR | | | 1980 PTR | | | Total of ranks | | | Rank of total | | |
|---|---|---|---|---|---|---|---|---|---|---|---|---|---|---|---|
| Sub-category | < 15 | 15– 17.4 | ⩾ 17.5 | < 15 | 15– 17.4 | ⩾ 17.5 | < 15 | 15– 17.4 | ⩾ 17.5 | < 15 | 15– 17.4 | ⩾ 17.5 | < 15 | 15– 17.4 | ⩾ 17.5 |
| F | 3 | 2 | 1 | 3 | 1.5 | 1.5 | 3 | 2 | 1 | 9 | 5.5 | 3.5 | 3 | 2 | 1 |
| H | 3 | 1 | 2 | 3 | 2 | 1 | 3 | 1 | 2 | 9 | 4 | 5 | 3 | 1 | 2 |
| J | 3 | 1.5 | 1.5 | 3 | 1 | 2 | 3 | 1 | 2 | 9 | 3.5 | 5.5 | 3 | 1 | 2 |
| R | 3 | 1 | 2 | 3 | 1.5 | 1.5 | 3 | 1 | 2 | 9 | 3.5 | 3.5 | 3 | 1 | 2 |
| K | 3 | 1.5 | 1.5 | 3 | 1 | 2 | 3 | 1 | 2 | 9 | 3.5 | 5.5 | 3 | 1 | 2 |
| Q | 3 | 1 | 2 | 3 | 2 | 1 | 3 | 1 | 2 | 9 | 4 | 5 | 3 | 1 | 2 |
| M | 3 | 1 | 2 | 2.5 | 1 | 2.5 | 3 | 1 | 2 | 8.5 | 3 | 6.5 | 3 | 1 | 2 |
| U | 3 | 1 | 2 | 2 | 1 | 3 | 3 | 1 | 2 | 8 | 3 | 7 | 3 | 1 | 2 |
| N | 3 | 2 | 1 | 3 | 1 | 2 | 3 | 1 | 2 | 9 | 4 | 5 | 3 | 1 | 2 |
| V | 3 | 1.5 | 1.5 | 3 | 1 | 2 | 3 | 1 | 2 | 9 | 3.5 | 5.5 | 3 | 1 | 2 |
| P | 3 | 1.5 | 1.5 | 3 | 1.5 | 1.5 | 3 | 1 | 2 | 9 | 4 | 5 | 3 | 1 | 2 |
| B | 3 | 1.5 | 1.5 | 2.5 | 1 | 2.5 | 3 | 1 | 2 | 8.5 | 3.5 | 6 | 3 | 1 | 2 |
| S | 3 | 1 | 2 | 2 | 1 | 3 | 3 | 1 | 2 | 8 | 3 | 7 | 3 | 1 | 2 |
| W | 3 | 1.5 | 1.5 | 2 | 1 | 3 | 3 | 1 | 2 | 8 | 3.5 | 6.5 | 3 | 1 | 2 |
| X | 3 | 1 | 2 | 1 | 2 | 3 | 3 | 1 | 2 | 7 | 4 | 7 | 2.5 | 1 | 2.5 |

# Appendix 6. Membership of groups

**A6.1 Monitoring team (NFER)**

The members of the Mathematics Monitoring Team at the NFER are responsible for constructing the mathematics assessments, marking the survey scripts and reporting on the results.

Mr D D Foxman (Leader)
Dr G J Ruddock (Deputy Leader)
Mr P Mitchell
Dr M E Badger (until Aug. 1981)
Mr R M Martini (until Nov. 1981)
Dr L S Joffe (from Nov. 1981)
Mr K P Mason (from Nov. 1981)
Mrs J Pengilly (Secretary)
Mrs R James (Clerical Assistant)

**A6.2 APU Steering group on mathematics**

| | |
|---|---|
| Mr T A Burdett HMI (Chairman) | APU |
| Miss J L Atkin HMI | HM Inspectorate |
| Dr A W Bell (until Feb. 1982) | Shell Centre for Maths Education, University of Nottingham |
| Miss M I Boland HMI | Department of Education for Northern Ireland |
| Mr D D Foxman | Leader, Mathematics Monitoring Team |
| Dr K M Hart | Centre for Science and Mathematics Education, Chelsea College |
| Mrs J M Holloway (until March 1982) | Fairlight Middle School, Brighton |
| Mr R L James (from Sept. 1982) | HM Inspectorate (Wales) |
| Mr G Littler (from April 1982) | Academic Registrar, Derby Lonsdale College of Higher Education |
| Mr I R Lloyd (until Sept. 1982) | HM Inspectorate (Wales) |
| Mr D J Maxwell | Education Department, North Tyneside |
| Mr P J Scott | Headteacher, City of Leeds School |
| Dr R Taylor | Head of Mathematics, Sudbury Upper School |
| Mrs D Walling (from April 1982) | Barden County Junior School, Lancashire |

**A6.3 Monitoring services unit (NFER)**

Mrs B A Bloomfield (Head of Unit)
Mrs A Baker
Miss S Darby
Miss E Elliott
Mrs M Hall
Miss E Evans (Secretary)

**A6.4  Monitoring group (NFER)**

Dr C Burstall (Chairman)
Mrs B A Bloomfield
Mr P Dickson
Mr D D Foxman
Dr T P Gorman
Dr W Harlen (Observer, APU Science Monitoring Team)
Dr D Omrani
Dr E Price
Mr B Sexton
Dr A S Willmott

**A6.5  APU consultative committee**

| | |
|---|---|
| Professor J Dancy (Chairman) | School of Education, University of Exeter |
| Miss J E L Baird | Joint General Secretary, AMMA |
| Mr P Boulter | Director of Education, Cumbria (ACC) |
| Mrs J Bushby | Councillor, Bromsgrove District Council |
| Mr P J Casey (up to April 1982) | Deputy Director (Education and Training), CBI |
| Mr R G Cave | Former Senior Education Officer, Cambridgeshire |
| Mr L Cooper | Deputy Headmaster, Sherburn High School (NAS/UWT) |
| Mr H Dowson | Deputy Headmaster, Earl Marshal School, Sheffield (NUT) |
| Professor S J Eggleston | Department of Education, University of Keele |
| Mr P J P Eley (up to April 1982) | National Confederation of Parent-Teacher Associations |
| Mr A Evans | Education Department, NUT |
| Mr G S Foster | Headmaster, The Towers School, Ashford (NUT) |
| Mr G Hainsworth | Director of Education Gateshead (AMA) |
| Mr K Hopkins | Director of Education, Mid-Glamorgan (WJEC) |
| Councillor P Horton | Sheffield Metropolitan District Council (AMA) |
| Mr C Humphrey | Director of Education, Solihull (AMA) |
| Dr K Jones | Parent and doctor, Sheffield |
| Mr T M Jones | Headmaster, Werneth Junior School, Oldham (NUT) |
| Mr J A Lawton | Kent County Council (ACC) |
| Mr G M Lee | Doncaster Metropolitan Institute of Higher Education (NATFHE) |
| Mr S Maclure (up to April 1982) | Editor, Times Educational Supplement |
| Mrs R Mills | Consultant Economist |
| Mr M J Pipes | Headmaster, City of Portsmouth School for Boys (NAHT) |

| | |
|---|---|
| Dr W Roy | Headmaster, The Hewett School, Norwich (NUT) |
| Professor M D Shipman | Department of Education, University of Warwick |
| Miss A C Shrubsole | Principal, Homerton College |
| Mr F A Smithies | Assistant General Secretary, (Education) NAS/UWT |
| Mr T P Snape | Headmaster, King Edward VI School, Totnes (SHA) |
| Professor J Wrigley | School of Education, University of Reading |
| Mr A Yates | Director, National Foundation for Educational Research |

# Appendix 7. Note on the APU

The Assessment of Performance Unit (APU) was set up in 1975 within the Department of Education and Science. It aims to provide information about general levels of performance of children and young people at school and how these change over the years.

The terms of reference of the APU are:

'to promote the development of methods of assessing and monitoring the achievement of children at school, and to seek to identify the incidence of under-achievement'.

Associated with these terms of reference are the following tasks:

1. To identify and appraise existing instruments and methods of assessment which may be relevant for these purposes.
2. To sponsor the creation of new instruments and techniques for assessment having due regard to statistical and sampling methods.
3. To promote the conduct of assessment in co-operation with local education authorities and teachers.
4. To identify significant differences of achievement related to the circumstances in which children learn, including the incidence of under-achievement, and to make the findings available to those concerned with resource allocation within government departments, local education authorities and schools.

The APU monitoring programme has been concerned to reflect the breadth of the curriculum in schools and to display the wide range of pupil performance. The assessment model adopted by the APU is based on a number of curricular areas. At the present time, monitoring is proceeding in mathematics, language and science, and the first survey of children's performance in their first foreign modern language will take place in 1983. The assessment of pupils' abilities in the field of design and technology is under consideration, but there is no commitment to monitoring in this area.

The assessment procedures in mathematics are developed by the Mathematics Monitoring Team at the National Foundation for Educational Research. The work is steered by a group consisting of teachers, advisers, teacher trainers, educational researchers and HMI. The work of all groups and the progress of the monitoring surveys is supervised by a small management team, which includes the administrative and professional heads of the Unit together with the chairman of each group. More generally, the APU is advised by a Consultative Committee, which is broadly representative of education, industry, commerce and parental concern.

In producing national pictures of aspects of pupil performance, the Unit does not report on the performance of individual pupils, schools or local education authorities. Survey results are published regularly, in the form of reports, by

Her Majesty's Stationery Office. This is the third report to be published on the mathematics performance of 15 year olds. The report of the third survey on the mathematics performance of 11 year olds was published in May 1982.

Further information about the work of the APU is available from the Department of Education and Science, Information Division, Room 2/11, Elizabeth House, York Road, London SE1 7PH.

# Index

An asterisk against a paragraph reference indicates that a definition or explanation of the term can be found in that paragraph.

(Note: A denotes Appendix)

Printed in England for Her Majesty's Stationery Office
by Albert Gait Ltd., Grimsby
Dd 717197 C30 11/82